Painkillers, Heroin,
and the Road to Sanity

Also by Joani Gammill

The Interventionist

PAINKILLERS, HEROIN, AND THE ROAD TO SANITY

Real Solutions for Long-Term Recovery from Opiate Addiction

• • •

Joani Gammill

HAZELDEN®

LIBRARY OF CONGRESS CATALOGING-IN-PUBLICATION DATA
Gammill, Joani, 1957
    Painkillers, heroin, and the road to sanity : real solutions for
long-term recovery from opiate addiction / Joani Gammill.
      pages cm
    ISBN 978-1-61649-521-3 (pbk) — ISBN 978-1-61649-528-2 (ebook)
    1. Opium abuse. 2. Medication abuse. 3. Heroin abuse. 4. Drug
abuse—Treatment. 5. Drug addicts—Rehabilitation. I. Title.
    RC568.O6G36 2014
    616.86'32—dc23
                                                    2014001285

EDITOR'S NOTE
To protect the privacy of those mentioned in this publication,
names have been changed and, in some cases, other details and
circumstances have been changed as well.
This publication is not intended as a substitute for the
advice of health care professionals.
Alcoholics Anonymous, AA, and the Big Book are registered
trademarks of Alcoholics Anonymous World Services, Inc.

18 17 16 15 14   1 2 3 4 5 6

Cover design by Jon Valk
Interior design by Cathy Spengler
Typesetting by BookMobile Design & Digital Publisher Services
Developmental editor: Sid Farrar
Production editor: Mindy Keskinen

To those people struggling with opiate addiction . . .
and to their loved ones

and to Father Martin, who is always with me

If you want to see a miracle, be a miracle.

- **Dr. Phil McGraw**

make many kids' worlds a better place. Alex's love for Max is endless, and his intelligence never ceases to amaze me (he is smarter than Lucy, but don't tell her I said that!). In the end, though, he is just a puppy that chewed up seven pairs of my sandals as I wrote this book!

My special friend, Ken, helped me with his support and love, not only in his encouragement in writing this book but by helping me navigate a tough year.

My nanny and heart, Stephanie, helped keep the kids and grocery shopping to a manageable level so I could finish this book. Thank you, Steph.

To Dr. Phil McGraw and all the wonderful staff on the *Dr. Phil Show*—in short, you saved my life. And, just as important to me as time goes by, your help changed the very direction of my life and gave me a *purpose.* Through that purpose you have given me the ability to go on to help others. The *Dr. Phil Show* has a huge and positive impact for many people. Thank you, Dr. Phil.

To the family of Kalli (not her real name), who you will meet in these pages, thank you for bravely sharing her story with me. I am sorry for your grief this past year. If her journey now has the potential to help others. I hope this gives you some peace.

To all the families who allow me into their lives every week to help them with their loved ones through the process of intervention, thank you for taking the road less traveled—always a more productive path.

Introduction

Be sober, be vigilant; because your adversary the
devil walks about like a roaring lion, seeking whom
he may devour. • 1 Peter 5:8

That passage from the New Testament warns about the dangers all people face in life, but to us addicts it has a special meaning. It speaks directly to our struggles with addiction, a disorder that stalks us all of our lives—threatening our health, our relationships, and our sanity—until we get the help we need to build a stable recovery lifestyle. Today, addiction to mood-altering substances is recognized by the medical community as a brain disorder, one that is widespread. With treatment and/or a peer support program, addicts can have moments, months, and years of reprieve, but like all other chronic, life-long diseases, active addiction can flare up again and require further help to get well. When such flare-ups occur, we call it a relapse. I hate the word "relapse." It conjures up failure, which as you're about to learn, doesn't have to be the case.

This book will focus on *"opiates,"* a class of drug that is plaguing our country and destroying lives in record numbers. You may have heard the term *"opioids,"* too. What's the difference? Opiates are naturally derived from the opium poppy; opioids are synthetic, or perhaps semi-synthetic—but they work in similar ways. This book uses both terms. But, because of the similar addictive potential, the term "opiates" is sometimes used more broadly, referring both to opium-derived heroin and to synthetic prescription painkillers such as oxycodone (OxyContin) and hydrocodone (Vicodin).

According to the federally funded 2011 National Survey on Drug Use and Health, about two million Americans are dependent on heroin or prescription painkillers.[1]

I am a recovering addict and an interventionist, I worked for twenty-five years as a registered nurse (RN), seven of those years in drug treatment programs. In this book, I challenge the conventional belief that if a twenty-eight-day rehab did not "work," it was a failure. Recovery from opioid addiction is a process, not an event. I am living proof that what some would deem as "failed" stints in rehab centers actually proved to form the building blocks of progress that would one day lead me out of the depths of opiate addiction. I received bits of wisdom from every rehab facility I attended that, even now, ring in my ears and come out of my mouth as I speak to others about recovery. The first of my many forays in rehab was at Father Martin's Ashley, a private treatment center in Maryland, and it is this bit of Father Martin's wisdom that continues to stay with me more than any other: "Once the bell has been rung, you cannot unring it." Getting well from this disease does not often happen in one event, one rehab, one detox, one Twelve Step meeting, or one outpatient treatment. As with some other diseases that require multiple forms of treatment, it can take many different treatment attempts and modalities to gain long-term sobriety.

In this book, I explore different approaches to recovery that motivate addicts to do what needs to be done to stay well. I look at the scientific explanations for the low rate of long-term recovery for opioid addiction and at what the strong, committed folks in recovery say are the challenges with sustaining recovery.

But science is only part of the story. I also share my own

struggle with opiate addiction and discuss the elements of recovery that I believe have helped me achieve my longest remission to date. I write about the commonalities I have seen between my struggle and the struggles of my intervention clients who suffer from opioid addiction. I also look back at some of the interventions I have done, helping addicts and their loved ones recognize the need to get help and enter treatment, and provide updates on how those patients are doing today.

I also examine the insurance industry and explain why standard benefits are inadequate to provide addicts what they need to get well from this destructive disease. Many individuals in our society still vilify the addict, but I believe that the real enemies when it comes to the proper treatment of addiction are larger and more powerful than any one person or group of people: a system that restricts access to appropriate health care and pharmaceutical companies willing to profit from the overuse and abuse of the prescription painkillers they promote indiscriminately. State resources are abysmal, and the rehabs they provide are not always successful; all too often they are more like revolving-door crash pads for detox only. Meanwhile, in 2011, U.S. sales of prescription painkillers amounted to $9 billion, according to IMS Health.[2] That says a lot about the health care industry's lack of oversight of the people who prescribe these drugs—and the role it plays in this addiction epidemic.

As I interweave the story of my own long love affair with opiates with the stories of others with whom I have come into contact, I offer hope to those who still struggle by illuminating what I feel to be the missing links to long-term sobriety. Opiate addiction is a complicated problem, but I believe that if we approach it from a new direction, we can help reduce the resulting carnage of the disease. The problem itself is huge, and I am under no delusion that I or any one person or approach

can s~ stroom to freshen up." We were all confused
arr ~restroom giggling. Freshen up? What did
~ she thought we needed to pee? We waited
~ought was the right amount of time and then
~merged, trying hard not to giggle. The woman was waiting
for us. She was not giggling; she looked too serious. She led us
to a room, where the men from the restaurant were sitting in
a circle on pillows with cards in front of them, playing poker.
The sweet and pungent smell of incense enveloped the room
and I did not like the vibe I was beginning to feel.

My friends and I were instructed to sit on pillows far behind the men to watch them play poker. Something was not
right—we thought *we* were going to play poker. Sitting quietly
and observing others is not the style of young American college women. Nonetheless, we sat and looked at another woman
wearing the same traditional dress as the woman who showed
us in. The men playing poker on this night seemed quite different from the men we had enjoyed at work. There they had
enchanted us with stories of old Persia. We would listen in-
tently, intrigued by those old stories told so expertly by our co-
workers who seemed to be natural storytellers. But now it was
obvious how little we knew of the men's home lives and were
not comfortable being excluded from the game. Watching the
men laugh and enjoy themselves as we sat quietly looking on
was not our idea of fun.

One man we knew better than the others was not playing
poker but was sitting on the floor close to the door on a large
mat. I went to him and said we would be leaving, that we were
not comfortable or having fun. He implored me to sit next to
him and listen to a story. He was the best storyteller.

"No, Ali, we want to go back to the dorm. Not tonight, save
your story," I said.

"Please," he replied, "we will smoke some pot. Bring the other girls over."

"Okay," I relented, "one joint and then we are going."

As we sat with Ali, the woman who had showed us in brought us hot, sweet tea. It had an unfamiliar, bitter aftertaste. As we sipped the tea, Ali loaded a pipe with a sticky-looking substance.

"Is that hash?" I asked.

"Yes," he replied.

I continued to sip my tea and remember feeling momentarily dizzy; I thought I must be hungry. The pipe now loaded, we passed it around. And that is my last memory of the night.

I woke in the morning to find that all of us—my friends and the men—were sleeping on the large floor mat where we had been sitting the night before. We were all naked. I was furious, confused, and scared. I woke my friends as I gathered our clothes. Dressing quickly, we left.

"Do you guys remember anything?" I asked, as we sped away in the Fiat. All of us had lost our memories, and all of our legs were sticky.

Never being calm-mannered by nature, I went to the restaurant that night. I got Ali to come out back. I had noticed that he was low on the totem pole of a strange hierarchy that existed among the men.

"What the fuck?" I asked.

"Calm down," he said, "it was just really strong Persian opium."

"You told me it was pot. And that tea?"

"Okay, I fudged the truth, but I did not want to scare you. It must have been really strong for you guys—you all passed right out."

"Yeah, and we all woke up with sticky legs, you son of a bitch!"

We never went to the police, naively thinking our use of the drug would get us into trouble, and we never returned to our jobs at the restaurant. We still do not know exactly what happened that night.

What I do know is that I had become one of the millions of people throughout history who had awakened in a haze from using opium or one of its many derivatives. It was only later in life that I understood the long-standing allure of the opium poppy and why it was called the "joy plant" by the Sumerians more than five thousand years ago.

It Begins with the Poppies

Archaeologists have found evidence of opium poppies at sites dating from as early as the ninth century BC. Early civilizations from the Sumerians to the Egyptians to the Ancient Greeks used the drug. The Sumerians, living in what is now Western Iraq, used it medicinally, calling it "the joy plant." They traded with their neighbors and so by 1300 BC, the Egyptians were not only using it but cultivating it on their own. In this way, the "joy plant" continued to be traded and used far and wide.

The Ancient Greek physicians Hippocrates and Galen wrote about the medicinal use of opium, recommending it for the treatment of such conditions as diarrhea, nausea, and insomnia. Galen even touted the drug as a sexual aid, but he was also aware that this was a drug one could overdose on. Alexander the Great's conquests in the Middle East led to the reintroduction of opium after the plant had fallen into disuse in the region. Some centuries later, opium would reach China via Arab traders.

In the 1500s, the Dutch discovered that opium could be smoked, and combined the drug with their tobacco. Eventually, the Portuguese would teach the Chinese the art of opium smoking, and it was adopted swiftly. Later, direct vaporization was used—think of a bong, or heating heroin on tin foil to create smoke that is inhaled; this leaves a black zigzag trail of heroin on the top of the foil. Trying to inhale all of the vapors from the heroin is where the phrase "chasing the dragon" came from. Direct vaporization is still the most common form used by opium smokers today.

For several hundred years, China imported huge amounts of opium. The Asian nation produced its own opium, but it was inferior to varieties its European trading partners provided. The English traded opium for Chinese tea and by 1800, Great Britain had a near monopoly on the opium trade with China. The Portuguese and the Dutch also exported it there, but their trade was small compared to the booming business of England's East India Company. As China's population doubled from 1750 to 1850, opium consumption rose steadily.

China outlawed opium in the 1700s but did little to enforce the law for the next forty years. When the country finally began enforcing the ban, the British still found a way to smuggle it in; this led to the first of the two Opium Wars with Great Britain in the 1800s. The Chinese were defeated in both cases. Today, many historians see these wars were more about trade deficits and economics than about the use and abuse of opium.

Meanwhile opium was beginning to create havoc in Europe and in America as well. Many of these problems stemmed from an alternate form of opium. Laudanum was a combination of alcohol and opium, usually in a syrup form that was invented in 1527. This elixir was used recreationally and for medical purposes; it enjoyed great popularity during the nineteenth and early twentieth centuries.

Morphine and Modern Pharmacology

In the early 1800s, a German scientist named Friedrich Sertürner made a momentous discovery when he isolated the main ingredient of opium, morphine. It was soon discovered that morphine was a very effective pain reliever and was also responsible for the euphoria so sought after by opium users. Sertürner's discovery launched the start of modern pharmacology and led to the eventual isolation of more than fifty distinct alkaloids from opium, more than from any other known naturally occurring drug.

At the beginning of the 1900s, most countries banned opium. Even before then, opium itself was not prescribed medicinally in western countries. However, morphine had become a common pain reliever and its use was common during the U.S. Civil War.

And the pills took off in America like a flood in a parched desert—a parched desert with too much money and modern pharmaceutical companies whose influence and power had grown over the years. Were those companies' motives to help people or to make money? It is probably a combination of the two, depending on whether you're talking about well-meaning scientists and other dedicated employees or some of the more avaricious executives and salespeople driven by ever expanding demand for growth and larger profit margins. Society can judge—and in some cases it has, in lawsuits brought against the companies for unethical advertisement and aggressive marketing of their narcotic products.

Retail sales of prescription opioids skyrocketed 127 percent between 1997 and 2006, from a total of 50.7 million grams of opioid medications (including methadone, hydrocodone [Vicodin], oxycodone [OxyContin, Percocet], morphine, meperidine [Demerol], and codeine [Tylenol #3]) to 115.3 million grams.[3] These statistics not only highlight the massive increase in the prescribing of opioids, but also the failure of the so-called war on drugs to reduce substance abuse and addiction problems right in our own backyard. One of the back-yards hardest hit, an area already suffering from economic challenges, was rural Appalachia and the Ohio River valley. Kentucky was one of the primary states that experienced a substantial increase in OxyContin sales and the related crime it generated. The crimes ranged from people illegally obtaining OxyContin by giving doctors false information about their health condition, to "doctor shopping" to acquire more of the drug, to pharmacies being broken into and robbed to obtain the drug. In all cases, the drug was often then sold illegally on the street. And because of the effect opiates have on the frontal cortex of the brain, the seat of the critical thinking necessary to recognize right from wrong, people's judgment is severely altered while under the influence of opiates. Look inside our prison walls—some studies say that up to 65 percent of inmates met the current standard for drug or alcohol addiction.[4]

· · ·

I was prescribed OxyContin following back surgery in 1997. My physician knew I was in recovery, and he told me it was the new pain medication given to people who have had problems with narcotic addiction. The doctor explained that the time-release action of the pill would keep me from feeling the euphoria that the addict in me was seeking. This was not the complete truth. Even when OxyContin is taken appropriately, meaning swallowed whole, eventually the pleasure pathway of the brain—the limbic system—will recognize OxyContin as a narcotic. Thus addicts' brains will still experience that aberration of the mind that sets us apart from nonaddicts, and the need for more narcotics will be activated (more about opiates, addiction, and the brain later).

THE BRAIN ON OPIATES

For those not afflicted with addiction, opium has many legitimate medicinal uses. But people unfortunate enough to have a genetic and environmental predisposition for addiction must run from it like it's the devil. The good news is that with recent advances in understanding the causes of addiction and its treatment, the secrets to successful recovery from opiate addiction are not that complicated.

Heaven and Hell

First let me say that my brain on opiates felt like pure heaven: euphoria and a sense of well-being enveloped my existence, and I felt truly happy for the first time in my life. But being on opiates also dragged me down into a state of absolute hell. Like most addicts, by the end of my using days, I was just trying to keep up with the amount of opiates my body demanded to not feel sick. This is called "tolerance", as a user physically needs more of the addictive drug just to function. Eventually I was as sick on the opiates as off; I was close to the end. The "jumping-off place" that the book *Alcoholics Anonymous* tells about was upon me.[7] I could not live with or without the drug—which is the point at which many addicts/alcoholics take their own lives. My heaven had turned to hell. The drug took away my passions and made me feel as though my body was possessed by an entity that wanted me all alone so it could strangle me to death.

My first experience with opiates occurred on that hazy night during college, but it wasn't until I was on the job as new registered nurse that I felt the powerful influence of the drug. Here I "diverted," a sanitized word for stealing, my first Percocet, which along with OxyContin (one of the common prescription painkillers prescribed today) contains oxycodone, a derivative of the opium flower. When I took this drug, I felt complete, happy, and confident for the first time in my life.

But fate had me move east, and I began working in the newborn nursery in a local hospital, where there were no drugs to steal; many years would go by before I used opiates again. Like a lot of opiate addicts, my use started with chronic pain caused by a back injury. I ultimately ended up having spinal fusion surgery and then became addicted to pain medications. Over the next ten years, I made many attempts to get sober with short in-patient stays at rehab centers, outpatient treatment, private detoxes, and just the sheer agony of trying to quit opiates on my own. Again fate interceded, and Dr. Phil McGraw, the psychologist and TV show host, did an intervention with me. This was the beginning of my sustained recovery. His was a no-nonsense approach of telling me what my future looked like if I stayed on the same path, the consequences if I did not agree to treatment. Very importantly, I was given the opportunity to undergo inpatient treatment for three months.

There have been multiple studies telling us that the longer addicts stay in inpatient treatment for addition to any drug, the higher the rates of recovery—but how many people can afford this type and length of stay? (Insurance coverage plays a huge role in our nation's addiction problem, a subject we will discuss in a later chapter.) Without intensive treatment that includes a rigorous recovery management plan, addicts will continue to experience intense cravings for opiates long after they stop using— cravings that lead to the high numbers of relapse. Even with many years off of opiates, I still feel the lingering need for them. For me, the cravings grow stronger at certain times of the year and I need to plan for this. Now, every fall you can see me riding my bike hard, with my Chihuahua, Lucy, in the front handlebar pack. While daily exercise is a part of my recovery plan, in the fall I increase the sweat. During this season, my cravings always set in, so off Lucy and I go on the bike. I run from the devil while blasting motivating music in my ears, telling myself that my brain is just playing tricks on me. Parking my bike by a recovery meeting, I go in and drink shitty coffee and sit among supportive people just like me. And for that day, I am safe.

It wasn't always that way. When I was under the influence of drugs, my ability to reason about right and wrong was completely misplaced somewhere in the chemical maze of my screwed-up brain (as we discussed earlier, opiates affect the functioning of the brain's prefrontal cortex). There's no more dramatic example of this than my continued use even after I had my first child. I also became a shoplifter when I was on opiates. It was easy: I was a new mom with a stroller, and there was lots of space in that stroller to slip things into. New moms are not profiled as shoplifters—at least they weren't until recently. My husband would come home, and I would proudly show him all the loot I had lifted that day. In my delusional state, I thought he would be impressed with the nifty skill I was developing and be proud of me! Instead, he would say, "Do you want me to come home and have to pick you up at the police station?" But I just did not get it: My drug-addled brain was unable to see the reasoning; I was temporarily mentally ill. Fortunately, with the help of my Higher Power and professional treatment, this condition was only temporary for me.

It was an ordinary morning when, as the sun was peeking over the hilly Texas landscape at the rehab center Dr. Phil had sent me to, a subtle but important shift occurred for me. I had been in rehab for six weeks, during which I vacillated between being emotionally flat and overly sentimental, breaking out in tears at odd moments. And then it happened. All alone in the community room that early morning, I heard a beautiful sound. It was music coming from the TV. The words elude me, but I remember how the melody affected me and I began swaying to its tune. As I closed my eyes, I got goose bumps—my passion for music was returning. I thought to myself, "Joani is coming home." It was a spiritual moment, like God was near and my brain chemistry was normalizing. Some cynics will say the experience was brain chemistry alone, but who or what unseen energy created that complex web of neurons in our heads? Is it science alone, atoms and molecules, the big bang—but from where? Everyone has an opinion.

The million-dollar question is this: Why do some people get addicted to opiates and others do not? Is an addict born or created? This is a question to which no one knows the definitive answer, but we've learned a lot about what predisposes some people to become addicted to a drug like heroin with their first use, while others can take it or leave it.

Why They Call It a Brain Disease

The brain is the control center of the human body. Drug use can change those parts of the brain that sustain our life and these changes can lead to the devastating behaviors we call drug addiction.

According to the National Institute on Drug Abuse, three parts of the brain are most susceptible to the ravages of drug abuse: the brain stem, the limbic system, and the cerebral cortex.

The *brain stem* controls critical life-support functions, such as the heartbeat, respiration, and sleep. Too much of an opiate, whether it be prescription drugs such as OxyContin or Vicodin, or illicit heroin, can cause brain stem functions to slow down. This means that your breathing or heart rate may slow down or even stop, and you die of an overdose. Also, if an opiate is combined with another central nervous system depressant such as alcohol, the effects on brain-stem functions may be exaggerated and simply stop working. This is what happened in the case of the tragic death in mid-2013 of Cory Monteith, a star of the television show *Glee*. The U.S. Centers for Disease Control and Prevention reports that 90 percent of accidental deaths by poisoning in the United States are due to overdose of opiates, which now rivals the perennial leader, car accidents.[8]

The *limbic system* regulates our pleasure center. When we feel pleasure from certain behaviors, we are motivated to repeat those behaviors, such as eating. In this way, the pleasure or reward center of our brains helps ensure our survival. The limbic system is also responsible for how we perceive emotions, both positive and negative. Drugs of abuse have the greatest effect on our limbic system, the reward center where learned responses take place. Interestingly, alcohol does not seem to create as strong of a learned response as opiates. Scientists believe this is because there is no analog in the brain for the chemicals released by alcohol to bind to in order to set up the conditioned

other drug use stimulates a greater release of dopamine than we would ever receive naturally. In this way, the reward center of the brain is "taught" to repeat the behavior so it can feel those feelings of euphoria again and again. Think of a candy you really like. From past experience, your brain knows it and so it releases a certain amount of dopamine when you eat it. When opiates are consumed, the brain inundates the system with dopamine—sort of like the difference between someone whispering in your ear or shouting.

If you repeatedly ingest drugs like opiates, your brain will adapt. It has come to depend on the large influx of dopamine from the drugs and so stops producing dopamine naturally. This adaptation has the effects of not only reducing or eliminating the feelings of pleasure we would experience through normal activities but also of creating a powerful motivation to use the drug—if only to feel normal. At this point, addiction has now taken hold.

When addicts suddenly stop putting opiates into their bodies and their brains have stopped producing their own dopamine, symptoms of withdrawal begin. Remember, dopamine is a basic neurotransmitter that controls many things in our bodies. Withdrawal symptoms can include lack of motivation, depression, sweats, diarrhea, and uncontrollable leg movements (which is where the phrase "kicking the habit" comes from). A sense of lethargy and a complete lack of positive emotions envelop the soul; it is almost indescribable unless you have experienced it yourself.

You might expect that the memory of this withdrawal would keep an addict from using a drug again once the brain returns to normal after a period of abstinence. Unfortunately this is rarely the case. The brain never completely forgets the euphoria that came with the mood-altering drug. Science calls this adaptation and conditioning. I call it the devil playing tricks on me. The remembrances are attached to "triggers," or things that were happening around the time the opiates were used, and experiencing those triggers can produce the urge to use again even after years of sobriety.

Here's what happens for me: Every fall as the air turns cool and pumpkins appear, I experience what my counselors described as euphoric recall. Science can explain my craving at this time of year for the high of opiates—the fall was when I first used them—but that does not make the desire for the drug any less real for me or for anyone experiencing this invisible need. It is a chronic illness that begs for daily management, like all other chronic illnesses.

The more heavily a person uses, the longer the abuse, and the younger the person starts using all affect how intensely the brain suffers changes and how long it will take to heal. When kids start using before the brain is fully formed in the early twenties, the potential is greater for lifelong problems with addiction. That is why it is so important to intervene as soon as the signs of abuse and addiction are apparent, the earlier the better. There is hope for recovery, however. Brain images taken one year after addicts became sober combined with behavioral support, such as a Twelve Step program, and in some cases pharmacological support, such as with antidepressants and anti-craving drugs (more about these later), reveal brains that had returned to normal.

Multiple Factors for Addiction

The National Institute on Drug Abuse reports that genetics strongly influence whether or not a person develops drug addiction—potentially increasing one's risk by an estimated 40 to 60 percent. This means that if your parents were addicted to alcohol or other drugs, you are much more likely to become an addict yourself.[12] Even so, genetic predispositions do not "make" anyone do anything and other factors play a role as well. Research suggests that environmental and social factors also play a part in addiction. Thus, two siblings may have the same brain abnormality correlated with addiction, but one becomes an addict and the other does not.

The question is made more complex by the fact that drug use alters the brain, which raises a chicken-or-egg question: Are people's brains different because they took drugs, or did they start taking drugs because their brains were different?

According to an article in a 2007 edition of *The Age* in England, scientists at the University of Cambridge reported that some people were predisposed to drug addiction because they seemed to lack the receptors for dopamine. The study concluded that the decrease in dopamine receptors rendered an individual vulnerable to addiction and was not a consequence of chronic drug exposure.[13]

Many addicted people also suffer from mental health disorders, especially mood disorders, and will abuse drugs to self-medicate their psychic pain. Again, there are many environmental factors that can strongly influence the use of drugs. If drugs are prevalent in school or, as in my case, at work—the hospital where I was a registered nurse had many addictive drugs around—the odds of abuse and addiction increase. We know that various kinds of child abuse and neglect, persistent family conflict, and other traumatic experiences in childhood can change a child's brain chemistry in a way that makes that person more vulnerable to addiction.[14] "The kids most likely to get addicted are the ones who also have other problems," said Dr. Mark Willenbring, director of the Division of Treatment and Recovery Research of the National Institute on Alcohol Abuse and Alcoholism, in an HBO special on addiction.[15]

Addiction professionals refer to the multiple factors that contribute to addiction—biological, psychological, and social—as the biopsychosocial model. Bill Wilson, cofounder of Alcoholics Anonymous, is whispering in my ear, "Body, mind and spirit," which are represented in the three sides of the triangle that is the AA symbol of recovery. I'm a living example of this biopsychosocial model of addiction. I had the perfect storm of risk factors for addiction: parents who set me up genetically, social influence of parents with addictive behaviors, school attendance in the 1970s on the heels of the drug culture of the 1960s, emotional health issues resulting from a mood disorder of general anxiety, and trauma from childhood sexual abuse. And yet, I am one of the lucky ones—lucky because I am beating the immense odds against me to stay sober today.

Trauma, I believe, was a big stumbling block in my ability to get well. I did not deal with the childhood issue of sexual abuse until my last rehab. In the next chapter we will look at the role that trauma plays in people's lives and treatments to relieve the brain's burden of the painful past.

3

TRAUMA, PSYCHIATRIC DISORDERS, AND ADDICTION

She is a small baby with lots of fuzzy blond hair. Her eyes, even as an infant, are that wonderful hazel color that changes with the light, sometimes amber, sometimes green—even her mood can alter her eye color. As a young child, she is already learning to bob and weave in this home burdened with alcoholism and dysfunction. She is full term but weighs barely five pounds. In the medical community, this is considered small for gestational age. The placenta had been robbed of vital nutrients that the growing fetus needed. Cigarette smoking by the pregnant mother created blood vessel constriction to the placenta and deprived the baby of blood and nutrition. The baby will have a compromised cardiovascular system that will last a lifetime.

By all accounts she is a "good" baby. She eats and sleeps well, cries little unless placed in her crib. Her phobias and anxiety that will last a lifetime start very young. She is petrified of the buttons in the crib mattress, thinking they are bugs that will harm her, and she becomes hysterical every time someone attempts to put her in the crib. Her babyhood is spent sleeping on the floor next to her parents' bed. Bath time can also be a challenge. If the baby sees a piece of lint or hair floating in the tub, she reacts the same way as she does with the buttons in the crib—she is convinced they are bugs that will harm her and panics to the point of having to be taken out of the tub.

Her next anxiety symptoms have to do with her feet. She will not take her socks off. She is convinced her feet are ugly and people will not like her if they see them. Starting at the age of three, she will never go out in public without her socks on. Then at age ten, yet another obsessive worry sets in. She is convinced that if she eats, she will choke and die. Sometimes swallowing her saliva can be a challenge. She will only eat liquids, and this becomes problematic for her weight. When she stays at a friend's house for a sleepover, her mom has to tell the family that she will not eat their food and to just give her liquids. The girl is embarrassed about her inability to eat, so she stops going to friends' houses. Isolation sets in. She has progressed to always wearing kneesocks, even in the heat of the Western summers.

Next the girl convinces herself that if she does not go outside and walk on every crack in the sidewalk, her mother will die. So every day, her job is to go outside in her kneesocks, having consumed only a powdered instant breakfast drink mixed with milk, and walk the sidewalks, stepping on every crack she can find. Her friends are playing and swimming and shopping, and the girl is walking the sidewalks, hungry and so afraid, and she has no idea why.

Her mom is worried that something is physically wrong with her daughter because she cannot swallow, so she takes her to a family practice doctor. After conducting a full physical, the doctor reports that she can find nothing wrong with the girl.

That is the end of assessments by any health care professional until she is fifteen.

At age eleven, she meets her new neighbors. This family seems to represent everything this troubled young girl does not experience in her own home. The family has two children, a girl and a boy, both around the same age and is of southern European origins. It is their tradition to be robust in their affection for one another. The father of this family is the opposite of the girl's father. Her father is excessively removed emotionally, showing no love at all to his daughter, and is a high-functioning, daily-drinking alcoholic, like his father before him. He provides food, shelter, clothing—all the financial necessities of life—but instead of love his presence delivers a great deal of fear. When the girl was younger, he assaulted her with a belt as punishment, and now she is always afraid of him. In contrast, the father next door is talkative, attentive, and sweet in disposition. The girl is drawn to him, unknowingly seeking what she is missing from her own father. It is the perfect breeding ground for a child predator.

Later, as an adult, the girl would come to recognize that the neighbor father was a prolific pedophile. He had honed his skill at grooming children to meet his sexual needs long before he met this new young victim. After seeing the family dynamics of a distant, unloving father, he knows that the girl will be easily manipulated into meeting his sexual needs. And she is.

He starts gradually, showing interest in her hobbies and offering friendship to the girl, always saying something positive to her about her appearance or an activity she is engaged in. He touches her in nonsexual ways, a hand on the shoulder, a quick hug when meeting. No one in the girl's life touches her. Hugs and "I love you" are never given or heard in her family. Her mother, addicted to cigarettes, tranquilizers, and beer, provides no support or buffer from her father's abuse. She is obsessed with her husband's needs; her main concern is his comfort, which includes maintaining complete quiet and distance from everyone in the family.

So this new neighbor offers the girl what she is starving for: love and physical contact. Ultimately, she is willing to let her childhood end abruptly by giving this man oral sex. His attention is like water to someone trapped in the dry desert, and the sexual part of their relationship goes on for years. When the girl enters adolescence, their relationship is discovered, and it ends. No legal action is ever taken, and the girl's family never approaches the man about the violation inflicted on their child.

The girl's anxiety now exhibits itself in not being able to be touched by the opposite sex. If a teenage boy shows interest in her, she won't allow him to kiss her or even hold hands. With any attempt at intimacy, panic sets in, and the relationship ends. She cannot attend high school dances because the thought of dancing with a boy causes her terror.

At age fifteen, the girl is diagnosed with hypertension, with a blood pressure of 180 over 100. Such extreme hypertension is unusual for a teenager, and the professionals are perplexed. After she is examined by a few experts, one doctor finally asks, "Did your mother smoke while pregnant with you?" She answers "Yes." The doctor asks if she was a small baby. Again, she answers "Yes." She is answering the doctor's questions quickly, hoping to end the examination as fast as possible. The proximity of a male doctor is causing her internal panic. The physician goes on to explain that her cardiovascular system may have been assaulted while she was a fetus, caused by maternal cigarette smoking, which has produced the subsequent hypertension. The girl will never tell her mother of this conversation with the physician, because she does not want her to feel regretful. What is done is done, and despite everything, she loves her mom too much to confront her with what is in the past.

To fight the hypertension, the girl is put on the tranquilizer Ativan. Maybe the doctor sensed her panic; the girl does not really know. This leads to her first addiction to a pill. Not only does the Ativan bring down the life-threatening blood pressure, it also takes away the debilitating anxiety she has had for most of her life.

But she has the genetic makeup of an addict from both of her parents. The tranquilizers awaken the sleeping giant of addiction, the genetic source of which had yet to be identified by scientists. Again, we now know that statistically the girl had a 40 to 60 percent chance of becoming an addict based solely on her family's genetic history. But in addition to genetics, other elements in her life combined to form the perfect storm of addiction: a mood disorder of anxiety, post-traumatic stress disorder (PTSD) from childhood sexual abuse, and soon, the social influences of other teens she had befriended who were experiencing similar life experiences and the drug culture they fostered.

PTSD and Sexual Assault

In a review of previous research on the subject, an article in the *American Journal on Addictions*[16] showed a strong correlation between female PTSD and early sexual and/or other physical assault. Women substance abusers in particular showed high rates of this dual diagnosis of a psychiatric disorder and addiction (30 to 59 percent), most commonly stemming from a history of repetitive childhood physical and/or sexual assault. We've known for some time now that understanding the relationship between addiction and repeated sexual and/or other physical assault is important in the treatment of women with addiction.

This article also confirmed what I have experienced and what many women have reported to me following an intervention: Women with a history of PTSD associated with sexual assault are more likely to be addicted to opiates and cocaine than to other mood-altering substances, such as alcohol or marijuana. The presence of trauma and PTSD that have been associated with addiction is called "traumatogenicity." The existence of this condition may be why women with a history of sexual and/or other physical abuse attempt to alleviate their suffering through self-medication. The journal article goes on to say that the relationship between addiction and PTSD also appears to be more enduring than the relationship between addiction and some other disorders, such as mood or anxiety disorders. The article also specifically connects the abuse and addiction to opiates and cocaine among women with PTSD from their childhood experiences of early assaults.

Again, this corroborates what I hear time and again from the injured and brave women I drive to rehab following an intervention. What I look forward to is the day when science discovers why certain drugs, like opiates and cocaine, tend to soothe sexual and physical traumas that linger in the injured brain more than other drugs. A disturbing fact cited in this multifaceted review of previous research is that PTSD symptoms are widely reported to flare up with initial abstinence of the woman's preferred drug, thereby triggering her to relapse. It has been hypothesized that these relapses occur because while the woman is free from mood-altering drugs, she can "feel" the past trauma. This raises the question, how do we treat this subset of women with histories of early assault?

• • •

It is an overcast day, and the respite from the summer Texas sun is both a treat and a gloomy harbinger of the woman's feelings that will surface later in the week. Decades have passed since the girl gave any serious thought to the sexual abuse that occurred when she was younger, if she ever gave it much thought at all. There was the time years earlier when she was talking to another young woman and the subject of oral sex came up. The details of the conversation are foggy now, but she remembers flippantly saying, "Yes, I was brought up on oral sex." Both of the women had laughed; both, it turned out, were victims of sexual abuse. And that was the end of the conversation.

The girl has been in rehab for two months now, battling addiction to three drugs—tranquilizers, opiates, and amphetamines. Her brain chemistry is returning to normal, and she has worked hard on her recovery, including a Twelve Step program. Every so often, gently, her female counselor brings up the girl's past sexual abuse. The girl provides glimpses of her past, but not in depth or with emotion. The counselor, whose instincts are razor sharp from years of working with injured women, knows it is time for the girl to deal with her traumatic past. Today, the girl told her about a dream she had the previous night. She could smell the perpetrator's cologne and felt terror as a phone rang just out of reach in her bedroom. The girl somehow knew that her mother was on the other end and over and over she tried to make her way to the phone, desperate for her mother's protection. But the girl could not reach her, even as she heard her mom's voice:

"Joani, where are you?"

"I am here, Mom. See me? Over here."

That girl was me and in the dream, my mom and I never connected.

Treatment of PTSD and Addiction

Prior to this dream, I had never had any "feeling" or experienced a breakthrough surrounding my sexual abuse history; I had never dreamt or thought of the abuse on any level. But as I continued my stay at this rehab, I would continue to face this demon and my one abiding feeling was anger. Anger is always a secondary emotion; hiding behind its fumes are the real instigators—hurt and fear. I was told by more than one therapist at this rehab that if I did not get to what was hiding behind my anger, I would have a hard time staying well.

I was tired. Tired of going to rehab. Tired of the anger and living a life that brought so much pain to me and my family. So one day, in a fury over something no doubt inane, I sunk to my knees and prayed in an outdoor spiritual sanctuary, high on a hill overlooking a bountiful valley with the Guadalupe River winding its way around. "Dear God, let me see what I am so angry about," I begged. I howled at the rising moon; I cried like a small child, with an abandonment that was primal in its absolute confusion and the need to see what was buried deep in my injured brain. Then, just as my tears cleared my eyes, I was rewarded with a glimpse of Ghost Kitty as she darted across my path. Ghost Kitty was a small, pure white cat, rarely seen, never touched, but very much a presence in this area. A good omen I thought.

That night I feel asleep listening to a distant owl. Deep in slumber, in that altered state of consciousness, I had the dream where I smelled my abuser's aftershave and was unable to reach the protection I needed from my mom. I was afraid, hurt, and alone. My prayer had burst open my heart to see the impossible. To remember the hurt, to begin to heal.

The next day, my counselor gave me an assignment: to write a lengthy description of the sexual abuse, all the specifics, the tiny details and feelings I could remember. On the assignment paper were many questions to help tease out the memories of my painful past. I wrote down my memories—sometimes sharp, sometimes foggy—while sitting in the shade of a large weeping willow. The tree seemed to hug me, and in the beauty and safety of this environment, I would finally let my memories flow, having gained strength from the support of the staff and the friends I had made in the strong community that forms when rehab is effective.

The specifics of those years of sexual abuse were not easy to put on paper. I felt embarrassed and somehow responsible for what happened, as if I had allowed it to transpire. But at my side was a picture of me at the age I was when the abuse occurred. This was part of the assignment, and as I lingered over the image of this young child, I cried for her and for her stolen innocence. I cried, too, knowing that my childhood lacked the love that a person inherently needs so as not to fall prey to sexual predators who take advantage of the emotional void that envelops such a child.

My therapist was having me write a "script" of what happened to me as a child. She would then use this script to lead my mind in a technique commonly called "guided imagery," a method used to treat PTSD that involves spurred memories and the patient's senses.

Other patients at the rehab had been through the scripting process, and we jokingly called it "mind busting," no doubt making light of it to ease our fear of going back in time. But back in time I went, in the hands of my well-trained counselor name Sunny. Her name would come to symbolize the results of our sessions together as I remembered and came to the other side of my painful past.

During the session, I sat in a chair. The room was softly lit and filled with the sweet smell of flowers. Sunny stood behind me and relaxed me with a soft touch to my head and shoulders as she took me into a kind of hypnotic state through guided relaxation. Then she talked to me of the experiences I had put to paper the day before. I was a child again, and the abuse and traumatic feelings of the time floated easily to the surface. Sunny helped me to feel the burn of my hate, to scream and cry. With all my feeling spent, I was free to finally forgive the man who abused me, to see him as a sick person, and to release the negative feelings I had toward him. Although the session had lasted about one and a half hours, during the experience time seemed suspended; I was in another place. When I walked away from that session, barefoot in a grassy meadow of sweet flowers, I could feel the cool grass on my toes. I felt the deep need to lie down and experience the softness of the field. It felt like I had entered heaven.

Later during my rehab, Sunny and I would have similar sessions concerning the ambivalent feelings I had about my father, who died in a car accident when I was seventeen; he had been driving drunk. I would deal with my fear and my hate, and ultimately reclaim my love and forgiveness of my dad. This would mark the beginning of my longest sustaining recovery and the loss of my chronic anger.

Another method of dealing with PTSD is called "eye movement desensitization and reprocessing" (EMDR). When I first heard of this technique, I was skeptical, and there is published literature and research that disputes its effectiveness. But other studies cite its usefulness and value. Beyond the conflicting literature, I have had the opportunity to talk with professionals and patients who have reported a high success rate in using EMDR to treat and diminish the effects of trauma on the brain. I have come to respect it as another possible tool in the box that can be helpful in dealing with the injured mind, a necessity for opiate addicts seeking lasting recovery.

EMDR was developed by Francine Shapiro in 1987. It is a form of psychotherapy based on the premise that traumatic memories get "stuck" in isolated memory networks in the brain. The theory is that the stuck traumatic memories are unable to be processed normally and linger in the mind, negatively affecting the person's mental health and in a sense traumatizing the person over and over in a vicious circle of unresolved trauma. EMDR involves a multistep process where patients focus on the negative memories while moving their eyes quickly from side to side, following the therapist's finger or an illuminated dot in front of them. This therapy is intended to stimulate bilateral brain activity and to get the mind to shift its thoughts bilaterally. When this occurs, the negative memories that are stuck in the isolated memory banks are freed up so they can be processed, dealt with, and dissipated.

Early in my career as an interventionist, I did an intervention with a woman who was a victim of childhood sexual abuse by her father and who chronically relapsed to abusing prescription opiates. She had lost it all: her husband, her career, her kids, her home. I would find her all alone in her small apartment, huddled in a fetal position in bed, many times with menstrual blood running down her legs. In her impaired state on opiates and suffering from depression, she had little awareness of her condition. She had made many attempts at sobriety at reputable rehab centers, and now her condition seemed hopeless. In one last attempt, I arranged for her to be taken to a local hospital by ambulance for a seventy-two-hour mandatory evaluation and detox. Afterward she agreed to another stay at a rehab, where she underwent EMDR therapy that focused on her memories of childhood sexual abuse. In 2013, she celebrated two years of sobriety.

There is a Buddhist saying to the effect that our complete failure and our greatest and final success sit side by side. Maybe it was a matter of timing with this patient, that she had had just enough failure at achieving lasting sobriety that success would finally be hers. Or could it be that she finally dealt with the most traumatic thing in her past, the thing that she kept soothing with opiates, and that EMDR helped loosen those stuck, painful memories in her hurt mind? In the end, it matters little to her kids, who got their mom back.

• • •

Scientists continue to look for ways to treat the suffering brain of addicts. Guided imagery and EMDR are just two techniques that have worked for some people who have buried traumatic events—events too painful to face until they reached a point when they are ready and the right people in the right place at the right time are there to help them. I have also seen negative attitudes, distorted perceptions, anger, and resentments abate in the continuing practice of Twelve Step recovery that includes working through the Steps in conjunction with peer support. "If we were to live, we had to be free of anger," Bill Wilson wrote in the book *Alcoholics Anonymous*.[17] While the care of an experienced mental health professional is recommended for people dealing with PTSD as a co-occurring disorder with addiction, doing the personal inventory recommended in Step 4 under the guidance of a skilled counselor or a seasoned sponsor can often help addicts deal with many kinds of traumas that have been buried in the past by their drug use. This is after working through Steps 1–3, since the Steps are designed to be worked in the order in which they were written. After we've admitted that we can't control our drinking and using in Step 1, we accept that we need the help of a power greater than ourselves in

Step 2; and in Step 3, we make the decision to turn our lives over to that power, which can be a God of our understanding, our treatment program, or the Twelve Step program itself.

We're then ready to work on Step 4—to take a searching and fearless inventory of ourselves. One key part of taking that inventory, as recommended in the basic text of AA, *Alcoholics Anonymous*, also known as the Big Book by AA members, is to write down all of our resentments and anger.[18] Then we look at our part in each situation that is behind those feelings. Often we find that we had something to do with what caused these feelings, including times when we personally caused someone harm, and in those cases we take responsibility for our actions in the Steps that follow; this includes preparing to make amends to the people involved—in essence, cleaning up our side of the street. But what if that other person really harmed us and we were the true innocent victim, like the pedophile who violated me? Eventually, through working the other Steps, often more than once, we reach a place where we can ask God as we understand God—our Higher Power—to help us forgive that person, just as I did with the pedophile who abused me when I was able to see him as a sick person, and show him tolerance and pity. Forgiveness is the imperative ingredient in all healing work done on trauma—both for the abuser and the victim. Bill Wilson, one of the cofounders of AA and the Twelve Step recovery movement, seemed to recognize that back in 1939!

Anxiety and Depression

Anxiety and depression are common co-occurring disorders (sometimes called "dual disorders") among opiate addicts, as they are with people addicted to other substances. These disorders need to be treated at the same time as the addiction if at all possible. Antidepressants, which are nonaddictive, are often prescribed along with psychotherapy. My chronic anxiety syndrome was finally addressed when, at the age of twenty-nine, I went to see a psychiatrist, Dr. James Kehler. I was at the point where I could no longer live with my psychological symptoms. I had been feeling an increasing sense of anxiety as a result of my drinking, which I had been doing to assuage my discomfort in almost all social situations. I also suffered from chronic insomnia and low-grade depression, commonly called "dysthymia." Dr. Kehler has now been a part of my life for decades and his care has substantially improved the quality of my life, in part by treating my chronic anxiety syndrome, social anxiety, and dysthymia with much-needed antidepressants that alleviated my psychological symptoms almost immediately. I am a living example of the importance of finding the right treatment program and the right mental health professionals who understand addiction and who can make the right diagnosis of co-occurring disorders and find the right treatment protocols that complement a long-term recovery management program.

And then my childhood angst returned through the eyes of my daughter. When she was eight years old, I began to see myself in her. She exhibited the same sorts of anxiety symptoms I had as a child. If we can recognize mood disorders in our children and get them treated, we dramatically decrease the odds that our children will turn to drugs and alcohol to self-medicate their psychological symptoms and discomfort. If they have the brain of an addict, we won't be able to prevent them from becoming addicts if they start abusing alcohol and other drugs, but we can lessen the chances that they'll ever start. I had my daughter evaluated and treated. We can only do our best to break the chain of generational illnesses through early recognition, intervention, and treatment of our children.

Of course, we must begin by protecting and loving our children so that they never experience the emotional or physical trauma that I and so many other addicts have had to deal with. It begins and ends with this: Love your children.

• • •

In the next chapter, we look at the dangerous new rise of an old adversary—heroin—as the restrictions on and reconfiguration of opiate prescription painkillers make them harder to get and abuse.

HEROIN

Old Enemy with a New Face

The parents of a New Jersey infant who died of heroin intoxication in 2008 have pleaded guilty to manslaughter after admitting they rubbed heroin on the baby's gums because he was teething. • Associated Press

The news is littered with some mundane stories and some outrageous stories, like the one above, about heroin overdose deaths and the increased use of heroin, particularly on the East Coast of the United States.[19] Sometimes we read the articles from afar, missing the feelings of the human element. The families affected by heroin and the devastation and death it causes suffer unimaginable frustration and grief. Their loved ones are taken by a disease that today is still often misunderstood, and many times relatives are not offered the same sympathy as if a sister, brother, mother, or father had been taken by cancer or another "respectable" disease. The general public continues to believe that there is "a choice" involved in addiction. But an addict with a brain predisposed to addiction does not have a choice. As Bill Wilson wrote in the Big Book in 1939, alcoholics "have lost the power of choice in drink."[20] Addicts do have the choice to enter treatment and do what needs to be done to stay sober. Although even this is not always easy from social, psychological, and economic standpoints, it can be done.

Kalli was twenty-five years old, and she loved to dance. I can imagine her blue eyes sparkling and her long blond hair swaying to the beat of the music. At one time in her life, she had passions: she attended the Philadelphia School of Fine Arts and loved animals, as well as her family. But heroin stole those things from her; addiction does that—it's a thief. Her parents, sister Susan, brother-in-law John, and their four beautiful and unique children lost a woman with a good heart and so much unmet potential when she died of a heroin overdose. Kalli was not what people typically think of when they think of heroin addicts. She did not have a troubled background and was not familiar with life on the street. In contrast, she came from an intact, upper-middle-class family that provided her with all the essentials needed by a child to lead a productive life. But as with cancer and diabetes, addiction is an equal opportunity disease, afflicting individuals with no regard to economics. It's just that the less economically well off who are on the streets as they scrape by to get the money needed to feed their habit are more visible and feed our convenient stereotypes.

The New Year's Eve revelry had barely ended the night Kalli was found by her boyfriend sitting upright and unresponsive on the couch in her living room. I wonder if she saw the ball drop at midnight in New York's Times Square before that unforgiving enemy, addiction, strangled her to death. We will never know. We do know that the boyfriend she lived with said he returned home that day in their only vehicle and found her intoxicated on alcohol. He said that she fell asleep on the couch around 9 p.m. and that her chest was moving and she was alive. He checked in on her again five hours later after having been asleep in their bedroom, and she was unresponsive, so he called 911. When authorities arrived, she was dead.

The police report makes me very sad, sad about the normal way they found her: sitting upright on the couch and wearing a long-sleeved pink T-shirt, blue jeans, one slipper on her left foot, and a blanket on the top half of her body. The small, gold crucifix on the necklace around her neck gave her no protection on this cold night. Her toxicology postmortem medication list reads like a pharmacy stock check-off sheet. Some of the medications prescribed to her could lead to claims of malpractice in the state I live in if the doctor knew she was an addict. Having read the autopsy report, I have no doubt that a combination of heroin, sedative drugs, and alcohol took Kalli's life. The autopsy confirmed my own conclusion by simply stating "Drug-Induced Death." As I write these words, I sometimes feel her presence in this room. Her gift to us is the cautionary story of her short life with heroin addiction and the real danger that this drug poses.

Just five months into 2013, Ocean County was matching the previous year's total number for overdose deaths, according to county prosecutor Joseph D. Coronato.[21] To understand the how and why of heroin use and overdoses there, we need to look at variables that make Ocean County vulnerable. The first variable affects not only Ocean County but a large part of the East Coast.

"Florida's crackdown on pill mills has dried up the supply of pills to much of the East Coast, with the unintended consequence of fueling heroin abuse," according to the blog Oxy Watchdog.[22] Then there is the geography of New Jersey that makes the influx of heroin easy. Ocean County, the largest county in New Jersey, is on the Atlantic Ocean east of Philadelphia and south of New York City. Ocean County is considered to be part of the New York metropolitan area. Much of the county is flat and coastal, with many beautiful beaches that draw tourists from up and down the East Coast and beyond. This is the good news for those looking for an ocean vacation, and for New Jersey, which needs tourist dollars. This happens to be good news, too, for criminals, who can slip into and out of the area looking like other tourists—tourists with backpacks full of tennis balls stuffed with heroin. Sometimes the heroin is smuggled into the United States in the stomachs of dogs that have swallowed packets of the drug. The packets are then cut out of the dogs, and they are left to die painfully after achieving their mission.[23] The "tourist" then throws a drug-filled tennis ball on the porch of a buyer who has deposited money in an online account that uses an alias name. Dealers and users are getting more sophisticated about hooking up; open-air heroin markets can be too conspicuous in quaint seaside towns.

Afghanistan is known to be the major producer of illegal opium, producing 87 percent of the world's heroin. Afghan opium, from which heroin and other drugs are made, kills 100,000 people annually, according to a report by the National Institute on Drug Abuse (NIDA) in 2011.[24] In 2011, the report said, 4.2 million Americans twelve or older (or 1.6 percent of the U.S. population) had used heroin at least once in their lives. It estimated that about 23 percent of individuals who use heroin become dependent on it. That information supports what the Philip Morris company knew about cigarettes in the 1950s and the NIDA report confirmed about heroin: the earlier you get a kid on drugs, the greater the chance he or she will have a lifetime struggle with the addiction.

The NIDA report estimated that there are almost 150,000

new heroin users each year. How many of them will become heroin addicts and require addiction treatment will vary each year, but this number tells us one thing with certainty: there is not enough education about the dangers of heroin and heroin addiction. No longer a drug considered to be the final stop on a long road of addictive behavior, heroin is now often one of the first drugs tried by youths interested in experimenting. From 1992 to 1995, the number of people who said they had used heroin in the past month rose from 68,000 to 216,000.[25] Every year since, that number has continued to climb. The age of first-time users has gotten increasingly lower, with more than 80 percent of them younger than twenty-six, which was once the average age.[26]

After first-time use, it takes only a few days of regular injection and a few weeks of regular smoking to develop a physical addiction to heroin. The average heroin addict will spend about $150 to $200 a day to maintain his or her habit, while many will spend even more. In less than a year, few can still be described as "functional" heroin addicts; that is, people who have a steady heroin addiction but still hold down a job or stay in school while paying rent and keeping up with other responsibilities. Instead, most heroin addicts are solely focused on maintaining their addiction and little else after the first year. As many as 50 percent of accidental and unexpected deaths are due to heroin and morphine use. It is estimated that as many as 150,000 emergency room visits each year in the United States are due to heroin addiction, equaling about 14 percent of all ER visits.[27] Those visits put an additional burden on our already floundering health care system.

The CDC reported in 2011 that deaths from prescription painkillers reached epidemic levels in the past decade.[28] What does this have to do with heroin? Teen use of prescription painkillers, which are easily accessible and are seen as a "gateway drug" leading to heroin addiction, has been growing in New Jersey, according to a state task force on opiate addiction.[29] That mirrors the growth seen in many other states around the country. Kids get started on the prescription opiate medication by simply looking in their own family's medicine cabinets. But prescription drugs are getting harder to obtain and have become more expensive. This is in part because of the increasing awareness by both law enforcement and society of the overprescribing of narcotics by health care professionals. The drug companies, under more public and legal scrutiny, have also made the pills resistant to crushing for snorting and shooting up. A few high-profile celebrities—Michael Jackson and Anna Nicole Smith—have died as a result of overdoses of prescription drugs, and their doctors are being held accountable.

Closing the door a bit on the availability of prescription opiate drugs has, however, opened a window for heroin to have a bigger impact on our society. When those who had used prescription drugs learn how much cheaper heroin is, and find they no longer need to play games with a doctor like lying and mimicking the symptoms of ailments they do not really have, or spend money on a doctor's visit, or leave a paper trail of their prescription usage (dealers do not keep good records), then bingo!—a new market share opens up to heroin.

I know from my own experience as an interventionist that the demographics among heroin users are changing. I never used to get calls like this:

"Hi, my name is Amanda, and I am calling about my husband."

"Please, what is going on?" I ask, hoping I sound as caring and empathetic as I feel. I know it is hard to make these calls.

"My husband, an executive at_____, is addicted to alcohol and heroin."

The first time I heard this over the phone about a year ago, I said, "Excuse me, say that again." It was so foreign to me to receive a call about this combination of alcohol and heroin addiction in middle-aged, college-educated men and women working in executive positions. In talking to such people in the car on the way to rehab, I started to hear a recurring theme. Heroin was now being used recreationally among this group, very much like cocaine was in the 1970s and 1980s. But unlike what followed three days of partying with cocaine, which most folks just slept off, the results of heroin use were different. Although the drug consisted of a fine white powder that looked like cocaine (most likely an attempt to draw in a new group of heroin users), after a long weekend party of snorting heroin, people were waking to a crushing and unexpected addiction to the opiate. It's estimated that of people who try heroin, about 23 percent become addicted, most likely because of genetic factors and their psychological profiles.[30]

With ever purer and cheaper heroin becoming more readily available and showing up on the party scene, more and more unsuspecting people are going to become addicted. Somewhere along the line, heroin's image has changed to that of a more "clean" drug, one not as feared in the past. This is what I hear in my car. "I thought it was no big deal—like a line of coke—but by Monday I was hooked."

The way to combat this problem is through education. I speak at schools near my home. The kids are great fun and are always brutally direct when asking me questions about my history with drugs and I always answer honestly. After every presentation I do, I invariably get four or five emails from kids who are addicted and need help but have been afraid to talk to anyone; I get them to the appropriate resources.

Although the time I spend at schools is well worth it, I do

get nervous right before I speak. Standing quietly, I silently say, "Dear God, let my words bring just one person home to sobriety." When I take what I am doing outside of myself into helping someone else, a strange calm descends, and I am able to speak.

When I think of Kalli and that crucifix around her neck, it takes me back to the days I worked as an RN at a state rehab facility. I used to sit in the parking lot in the predawn hours listening to Sarah McLachlan's song "Angel," hoping I could bring some comfort to my patients. I never knew Kalli, and yet, I know her well. Now, when I listen and hear the words "You're in the arms of the angel—may you find some comfort here," I think, "*From one addict to another, this is for you, Kalli.*"

5

MONEY, MONEY, AND MORE MONEY

The Salvation and Curse of Prescription Drugs?

"Please come quick," was the urgent request I received from a male voice on the phone. "I have heard you help folks with prescription drug problems."

"I do," I answered, elaborating, "I help by doing interventions and getting the person to accept the help of rehab."

"It is too late for that. I can't get her out of bed."

"I have done many interventions sitting on the person's bed," I said, and it is true.

"She is not responsive," he replied quickly.

"Maybe you need to call 911," I said.

"No, she has been like this for about three months," was his unexpected reply.

"So why is it urgent now?" I wanted to know.

"She went to a new doctor, and they increased her pain medication. Now I am afraid she will get less responsive."

"Oh, so she does get out of bed to get to the doctor then?" I asked.

"Yes, she has fibromyalgia and is on a ton of medications."

"Is she getting any better from the medications?" I asked, even though I knew the answer.

"No, she is getting worse."

I always listen to my gut. Normally I would have had him go through the usual channels of setting up an intervention, but a small voice was whispering in my head.

"Where do you live?" I asked, knowing intuitively before he answered that he lived close to me—and yes, he lived maybe two miles away.

"Okay, I will be right over," I said, to his surprise.

"Awww . . . great, see you at the front door." Then, as an afterthought, he asked, "How much do you charge?"

"Nothing; this one is on me," I said.

My gut was telling me something more. For some reason, I didn't see this as a formal intervention to plan, although it would have been easy to lead this gentleman in that direction. My inner voice was telling me something else, but what?

False Promises

It was an overcast day in early autumn. This was my favorite time of the year but, as I've discussed earlier, also my most dreaded because of the conditioned learning that my brain created while I was first using opiates, which was in the fall. This conditioned learning, also known as a trigger, leaves in its wake an intense craving for opiates every autumn.

I drove my van down a long, winding road, wondering how I had missed knowing this secluded neighborhood was here. The house was behind a grocery store that I frequent. Paul, the man who had called, told me he would be waiting for me by the front door. I suddenly realized I did not know the name of the woman I was to meet. I was also aware that I should be cautious in approaching this situation. A man I didn't know had gotten me to come to a home in a secluded neighborhood to check on his wife, whose name I did not know. It is written in *Alcoholics Anonymous,* "Keep on the firing line of life . . . and God will keep you unharmed."[31] I sure hoped so.

The house sat on the side of a hill down from the road. The leaves were still on the trees, and more than the average amount of foliage covered the house and the surrounding area. It gave the outside of the house a very dark feeling, foreboding almost. In the front of the home, though, was a lovely pond, and I could hear a pleasing trickling sound as my Chihuahua Lucy and I got out of the van.

As promised, Paul was waiting for me.

"I can't believe you came. I have been so worried and I just don't know what to do," he said.

Before I entered the house with a strange man, I wanted some sort of confirmation.

"Who did you get my name from, Paul?"

"A therapist I have been seeing."

After he told me the therapist's name, I felt confident about going in to assess the woman. I know the therapist well and have received several referrals from her. We walked into the house together. The home was immaculate. The beautiful wood floors had a deep, dark shine, and the hallway clock chimed the noon hour.

"Come," Paul summoned, "she is upstairs in bed."

We climbed one flight of stairs to a landing before climbing one more short flight. The area felt like a loft; you could see down to the living room from the landing. The carpet on the stairs was pure white, and because Paul had asked me to take my shoes off at the door, I could feel its softness on my feet.

We walked into what looked like a sickroom. On both

nightstands were pills, some in bottles, some lying about in silver dishes. Sitting on the floor was a box of pill samples with the name tramadol on it—the type of box those fancy drug representatives give out to doctors' offices to push their newest products. Tissues were strewn about, a breakfast tray lay on an ottoman off to one side, and a crumbled newspaper was on the floor. There was a huge, disheveled comforter on the bed, and a cat was napping at the foot of the bed. "The woman must be very small," I thought, because I saw no one on the bed. She must be under the comforter. I gently sat on the bed, letting Lucy loose. The cat immediately found different quarters. First I laid my hand gently on the top of the comforter, signaling my presence to whoever was under the pile of down. Then I pulled back the comforter and was rewarded with the sight of beautiful blond bangs. Big blue eyes slowly looked up at me.

"Hannah?" I whispered my surprise, disbelief, and sadness. "Is that you?"

My old friend gave me a weak smile. I recognized her face, but illness had shrunken it into a skeletal mask. I used to know Hannah well. We had attended AA meetings together, and she was a mentor to me early on in my recovery. She had a long history of heroin addiction and strong recovery. Now she was huddled on her right side in a fetal position and was so small she looked like a child.

"Give me a hug, honey. Things don't look so good in here," I said. She turned over just in time to get some Lucy love, as my dog moved in for a kiss before me. "Your dog," Hannah said, as she scooped up Lucy in her bony arms. Then her arms went around my neck and she cried as I patted her hair. I felt as if I was comforting a dying child.

As someone who always gets to the point, I asked, "Hannah,

what is wrong?" I had not seen her for perhaps two years. Her voice still had that signature, gravelly sound that I remembered, maybe from years of smoking. She was still pretty, but the wrinkles on her shrunken face were unnaturally deep. She turned onto her back slowly, like an elderly woman, not the youthful fifty-year-old I remembered.

"Well, first I was diagnosed with fibromyalgia for a few years and was in unremitting pain. They finally figured it out that it was Lyme disease from a tick, no doubt from all these fucking trees around the house."

"What did the doctors do for the Lyme's?" I asked.

"I was on a long course of different antibiotics for almost a year. Because it was diagnosed late, sometimes I was on intravenous antibiotics."

"So what are they saying now?"

"That I am pretty much cured, but in the meantime I have gotten addicted to the opiate pain medication."

"Did you tell the doctor of your heroin history?"

"God, no. I can't take that prejudicial judgment crap they give you."

I knew how she felt. I have had doctors dump me as a patient when I had trouble with my addictions. Even though the American Medical Association considers addiction, including alcoholism, to be a brain disorder, prejudice about the disease continues.

"Okay, Hannah," I said. "I get that, I really do. But for God's sake, you have had a huge, long, hard history with heroin. Your room here looks like a pharmacy. The Lyme disease is under control, but it does not take a PhD in addiction science to see what is going on here. You are playing the pain game with the doctors to feed the monster. Am I wrong?" I asked, challenging her.

Health Care: A System Gone Awry

In reality, Hannah was not the only one at fault for the collections of opioid pain medication I saw scattered around her room. Many times we vilify addicts for their prescription drug problems when there are other culprits. Most people might assume I would put doctors at the top of this list because they are the ones who write prescriptions for pain medication. But the managed care health care system that emerged in the 1970s drastically changed how doctors deliver medical care to patients.

Managed care's original goal was to contain the escalating cost of health care in America by working with insurance companies to oversee medical treatment, regulating the health care prescribed, such as length of stay in treatment facilities and hospitals, at times mandating alternative treatments to those originally prescribed, and sometimes completely denying a treatment prescribed by a doctor, again in an attempt to hold down costs. Managed care is now nearly universal in the United States, but it has become controversial because it has largely failed in the overall goal of controlling medical costs. What it did do was take away much of the control and decisions that doctors had in treating their patients. They had to deliver their medical care faster and cheaper to get paid by the insurance companies' managed care system.

Having been a nurse since the 1970s, I have seen the system change dramatically. Today, instead of waiting and seeing if the patient might need pain medication, too many doctors give out the script *just in case* it is needed. Most doctors do not have the time to see the patient again or receive lengthy phone calls about the patient's progress. Again, the managed care system squeezed what were for the most part well-meaning, hard-working doctors into changing the way they practiced medicine. The more pain medication that was prescribed, the more the public began to rely on it and began to see its use as the norm.

For example, a sixty-year-old woman goes to her doctor because she has started to have nagging and persistent pain in one of her knees. The doctor examines the knee and cannot feel or see any specific orthopedic problem and correctly diagnoses osteoarthritis of the knee. Nonsteroidal anti-inflammatory drugs (NSAIDs) work well for this sort of pain, as do lifestyle changes and physical therapy. But the doctor is under the gun to see so many patients in a day. He has been put on the managed care treadmill, where doctors have little time to talk about the patient's lifestyle, exercises they should be doing, or weight control. So out comes the prescription pad. And just in case the anti-inflammatory drug does not work well enough, here is a script for Vicodin, an opiate pain reliever with hydrocodone as its main ingredient. The doctor does not have time to be bothered by phone calls from the patient saying the pain is not being helped by the anti-inflammatory medication.

Under the managed care model, patients have all but come to expect opiate pain medication as part of the quick-service medical care we receive. Things have gotten better recently with all the bad press about the opiate epidemic, but there's still a lot of overprescribing for convenience going on. I've said it before, and it's worth repeating: Americans make up 5 percent of the global population and we consume over 80 percent of opioids worldwide.[32] We are the opioid nation. And guess what happens to many of the bottles of narcotics that adults never use? They remain in medicine cabinets and are ripe pickings for teenagers at the age of experimentation. And, as you read in the previous chapter, here starts a whole new problem that usually leads to heroin use. Sooner or later Mom and Dad's medicine cabinet empties out and heroin that is cheaper, very pure, and therefore more dangerous has become easy to get.

Others at fault for the increase in the misuse of prescription pain medications are unethical doctors and so-called health care entrepreneurs. Meet twins Christopher and Jeffrey George. They opened their first of four "pain clinics" in a Florida strip mall in 2008. They needed doctors for this clinic. An advertisement on craigslist connected them with a deluge of physicians willing to work for them. By the end of their heyday, the doctors, the twins, and the pharmaceutical companies had all made millions pushing legal opiate narcotics, for cash only. No insurance accepted. That kept the paper trail to a minimum.[33]

In spring 2010, the George brothers were the target of Operation Oxy Alley, an investigation into pill mills in Broward and Palm Beach Counties. Local and federal police raided their businesses, confiscated their opioids, and seized assets worth millions, including safes full of cash stashed in the attic of the twins' mom, according to prosecutors. In August 2011, the U.S. Department of Justice unsealed a five-count indictment outlining a range of charges, from racketeering to possession with intent to distribute controlled substances, against thirty-two people, including thirteen doctors and one wholesaler involved with the Georges' clinics. From 2008 to 2010, according to federal agents, the twins were the largest illegal dispensers of oxycodone in the United States.

Pill mills continue to spring up, take home the cash, go offshore, and are never seen or heard from again. But it is getting tougher. Federal and state governments, and law enforcement in the United States, are feeling the heat of the increasing problem of addiction to prescription drugs and the overdose deaths it is causing. They are cracking down with tougher laws and sanctions.

Still, OxyContin (oxycodone) racked up more than $2.8 billion in sales in 2012, even after the high-profile lawsuits and settlements claiming the company had misrepresented the addiction potential of the drug.[34] In May 2007, the maker of OxyContin, Purdue Pharma, and three of the company's executives pleaded guilty to misleading the public about Oxy-Contin's risk of addiction and agreed to pay out more than $600 million in one of the largest settlements involving pharmaceuticals in U.S. history.[35] Its president, top lawyer, and former chief medical officer pleaded guilty as individuals to misbranding charges, a criminal violation, and agreed to pay a total of $34.5 million in fines. Those three top executives were charged with a felony and sentenced to 400 hours of community service in drug treatment programs. I think it would have been tough for them to work in a drug treatment program, not just because of the troubled people they would have encountered but because some of those people may have been harmed by their drug.

I was one of those folks who was hoodwinked by Oxy-Contin. After my spinal fusion surgery, my physician prescribed OxyContin for me, saying, "It is nonaddictive and safe for a person with a history of drug addiction to use for pain control"—repeating, no doubt, what a drug rep had told him. The snake-oil salesmen of yesteryear, touting the benefits of cough syrup laced with sherry and opiates, is still with us today; they just dress fancier and carry better briefcases, loaded with samples of the latest, best, and brightest addictive drug.

Tramadol was another pain medication that flooded the U.S. market in the not-so-distant past. Tramadol was patented and licensed out by Grünenthal GmbH, a family-owned German pharmaceutical company formed in 1946. The company is well known for the development and sale of thalidomide, which caused birth defects in infants when women took the drug for nausea during pregnancy in the 1950s and 1960s. In 1995, tramadol was approved for marketing in the United States as a noncontrolled analgesic under the trademark Ultram. Although Grünenthal GmbH originally claimed that this substance created only very weak narcotic effects, recent studies show that opioid activity is the overriding provider of the drug's pharmacological potency. Because of inadequate product labeling and lack of established abuse potential, many physicians felt this pain reliever was safe to prescribe to recovering narcotic addicts and to known narcotic abusers. Of note, it is insanely easy to obtain on the Internet.

Tramadol sent me back to rehab, hoodwinked again. I took my first tramadol as I sat at a roundtable regional PTA meeting for my kid's school in 2006. My right leg and hip were hurting after sitting for a lengthy period, and I thought the painkiller would help. About fifteen minutes after I took the pill, I knew the drug was acting like an opiate on my brain. Two minutes later I was in the bathroom, where all drug addicts end up at some point, frantically searching my purse for another tablet to take, in private. The good news is that I had had such a good recovery after my previous stint in rehab, which lasted three months, that I did not indulge this relapse for long. Instead, I called the people at the *Dr. Phil* show, and within fifteen minutes, my good friend and producer Stephanie Granader had a solution: "Hang on, we are coming." I was quickly whisked back to the La Hacienda rehab center in Texas.

A group of us in rehab had been given tramadol and told it was safe despite our addiction to opiates—and we had all quickly become addicted to it. Numerous reports of abuse and dependence on this drug have since been made public. Tramadol is not a federally controlled substance in the United

States, but as of this writing, eleven states—Arkansas, Kentucky, Illinois, Mississippi, New York, North Dakota, Ohio, Oklahoma, Tennessee, West Virginia, and Wyoming—and the U.S. military have classified tramadol as a schedule IV controlled substance, having a low potential for abuse. Other states have legislation pending that would reclassify tramadol, a drug which earned Grünenthal GmbH more than $152 million in 2012.[36]

So are the pharmaceutical companies money hungry drug pushers, or are they researchers and developers of life-saving drugs? In reality, they are both. But just as Philip Morris misrepresented cigarettes to the public in the 1950s and Mead Johnson and other baby formula companies succeeded in getting a whole generation of women to believe that formula was superior to breastfeeding, there were big and powerful pharmaceutical companies misleading consumers again, and they played a huge part in creating America's opiate addiction epidemic.

• • •

"Hannah, what can I do to help?" I asked, as I looked at the huge box of tramadol on her floor.

"Do you still love me?" she asked.

I laid my wet cheek on hers and whispered, "With all my heart. Do not be ashamed, Hannah. You are sick, not bad." I whispered with a conviction I felt to the depth of my being. She was me, and I was her—we were both still misunderstood addicts. We must love each other because so many outsiders still don't understand our struggles that so many times happen in silence and solitude out of shame. A shame that should not exist in our supposedly enlightened times, but it does.

Through her sobs she said, "Help me get to rehab."

And that is what I did. Today, Hannah lives in a warmer state. I hear through her sister that she is doing well.

My instincts on the day Hannah's husband called were right on. And I also believe that God was near.

• • •

I've quoted the statistics before but they bear repeating: The number of unintentional overdose deaths per year involving opiate pain relievers such as oxycodone and hydrocodone nearly quadrupled from 1999 to 2007, rising from 2,900 to 11,500, according to the U.S. Centers for Disease Control and Prevention (CDC). In 2009, the death toll soared to 39,147, surpassing for the first time traffic accidents as the leading cause of preventable deaths. Two years later, in 2011, the CDC declared prescription drug overdoses to be an epidemic.[37] Opiate addiction is an epidemic that demands treatment that many people cannot access or afford. In the next chapter, we will look at the restrictions that currently exist in treatment availability for addiction and how we can work to open the door for those with limited resources and special needs. It is not always easy.

6

THE DOOR IS CLOSED

Barriers to Addiction Treatment and How to Overcome Them (Sometimes)

As the next two case studies illustrate, it doesn't matter what we're addicted to: getting into the right treatment program—or *any* treatment program if you don't have the money or right insurance—can be a challenge. That's true even when the drug is alcohol, still the most abused substance around the world. Many opiate addicts are also alcoholics since both drugs are depressants, although not all alcoholics are necessarily addicted to opiates and vice versa.

• • •

"My mom is really sick," was the first thing this concerned son, David, told me on the phone.

"Tell me more about your mom," I said, and as usual, I was surprised that a complete stranger would share such intimate details about his family members and himself. I like to think it is the empathy and concern in my voice that motivates them to talk to me, but I sense it is a deep desperation about the situation that spurs them on. By the time you need an interventionist, the situation has usually reached a crisis point.

"She is drinking all day and night, pretty much passed out a lot of the time," he said. "She fell the other day and got pretty banged up." One of the most common ways alcoholics die is by falling, hitting their heads, and suffering a fatal head trauma.

"How old is she?" I asked, needing the basic information to do my job.

"She is sixty-five; she just retired. She worked for a department store for forty years."

"Wow," I said, "a long time. What was her job there?"

"She worked on the floor, mainly working sales in the kids department," he told me.

"How long has she been retired, and tell me, has the drinking escalated since her retirement?" I knew the answer to the second question before I asked it. I see it a lot. Some functional alcoholics with responsibilities to jobs can keep their drinking in check. But when there is no more clock or boss to answer to, the drinking quickly escalates. That, and the person's social system has changed as well. The subculture of work buddies is no longer available on a daily basis. When life situations change, addictions can flare up like a forest fire out of control.

"She retired about six months ago, and since then the drinking has gotten progressively worse."

"Okay," I said. "Tell me, is your dad around, or does she live alone?"

"She lives alone. My dad has not been around for a long time." His voice lowered an octave with this admission, and I sensed some sadness there. But I am not a family therapist. My main goal was to get his mom to treatment. Not that I am not empathetic toward family sadness—I am—but time was limited, and this woman needed help quickly. The family programs at rehabs deal with the family dynamics.

"Who gave you my number, Dave, and does your mom have any other health issues?" I asked next. I was trying to get a handle on what rehab center would fit this patient.

He told me the name of the rehab facility that had given him my number. It is a wonderful rehab but can be costly. "She does not have any other major health concerns, some minor hypertension," he said.

"Does your mom have insurance or resources for rehab?" I asked. "I don't presume to know your finances, but that rehab is expensive for most people."

Then my heart sank. "She had pretty good private insurance when working but is now on Medicare/Medicaid since her retirement." Crap, I thought. "We don't have much money. I am her only son, and I do lawn work." Crap again.

In 2013, Medicare and Medicaid paid for detox—inpatient detox at times—but rehab was rarely covered at all. Not covering and making available rehab to the newly sober denies them the most important part of getting well from alcoholism and addiction: learning how to *stay* sober. The psychological issues and diagnoses that are almost always present with addicts need to be addressed and treated. Detox is like mowing over the weeds; rehab is pulling the weeds out by the roots. Detox only is like pissing in the wind. This woman needed way more than a detox, but that was all her government insurance would cover, after she had worked her forty years on her feet selling children's clothes and supporting her son.

• • •

It was the day before Christmas Eve, and I received a call.

"My name is Jeff. I am just home from Iraq on an earned holiday leave."

Nobody from the armed services ever calls me to tell me they are on leave, so I immediately realized this was a business call.

"What's happened, Jeff?"

His voice cracked as he said, "I came home and found my wife passed out in our driveway from alcohol. We have three little girls who were in the house hysterical. I have called Tricare, our insurance carrier for enlisted families, and can't get anywhere!"

"What do you mean you can't get anywhere?" Again, I knew the answer. I have heard this before from other service families.

"They transfer me from department to department telling me I have to get her to a place far from here for an evaluation to determine level of care, but they are not available until after the holiday. And we cannot afford the local hospital."

He was frantic. His three daughters were under the age of six and his wife was very ill and it was Christmas. He was scheduled to return to Iraq right after New Year's.

He mentioned one rehab that Tricare said he could take her to, but unless you brought along a can of bug spray for the cockroaches and a Taser for the criminals, I couldn't recommend it.

Making Drug Rehab Accessible

We are apparently the greatest nation on the globe, and yet our health care is just woeful on so many levels. I recently read an article about the Patient Protection and Affordable Care Act, better known as the Affordable Care Act (ACA)—or as it's come to be called, Obamacare—and I got a headache. There was so much verbiage that I found it confusing. But my understanding was that addiction/alcohol rehab will be available under the law if you qualify. The ACA names alternatives that can be pursued first, mainly outpatient treatment, counseling, and social skills programs. The thought that the government—a government worker—will have the power to decide if I or any of my patients qualify for life-saving treatment scares the hell out of me. I am sure there will be boxes to check off on some form, but the determination can still be very subjective. People can have harsh feelings about alcoholics and other addicts depending on their own personal history. This bias based on a government worker's life experiences could have a negative effect on the addict seeking treatment, as the worker has the power to determine the level of care that person should receive.

Maybe I am being too negative—or maybe I am being realistic. Time will tell. Patients will still have the option to carry private insurance, so I assume that for those with absolutely no alternative, ACA could fill in some gaps in health care. In a 2013 interview on CNN, U.S. Health and Human Services Secretary Kathleen Sebelius reported that nine out of ten people who needed mental health and addiction treatment in this country did not receive it in 2012.[38] What she said about ACA gives me hope that it will require better coverage of treatment services for addicts. Time will tell—let's hope it happens. One very excellent benefit under ACA is that young alcoholics and other addicts will now be allowed to stay on their parents' private health insurance until age twenty-six with no stipulations like having to be in college. Even with private insurance, a patient rarely gets a whole typical rehab stay (twenty-eight days) paid for at the best facilities. If the rehab is in-network, every few days an intake counselor must obtain clinical information on the patient to pass on to the insurance company. Depending on how the company deciphers that information, it will either approve paying for a few more days or it will deny further coverage.

When you look at your insurance policy, look closely; it usually says the insurance company will pay 100 percent of the *allowable* charge. "Allowable" is where they get you. Let's say the rehab costs $450 a day, but your insurance company allows only $200. You will come out with a hefty bill. Before admission, most respectable rehabs will give you their best estimate of what they feel the charges will be. Some nonprofits have funds that will cover any additional costs under certain conditions. Sometimes this is just a ballpark figure; it is tough to say with some insurance companies beforehand what will be paid. And this can make it difficult for people with limited resources.

• • •

My next question to David about his mother was, "Does she have a retirement fund? You can use that money for emergency medical services without taking a tax hit."

"Yes," he said, "she was very diligent about putting money away for retirement."

The way David's mom was going, she wasn't going to enjoy those retirement funds. It was a better investment at this point to use that money for her health.

David agreed. He had previously gotten power of attorney over his mother's affairs, which made it easy to access the funds. I also spoke to the rehab center and described the woman's financial situation and was able to get her a discounted rate. Remember, *always* ask for a discount or scholarship if money is an issue. You would be surprised at what you can get sometimes.

Insurance companies consistently deny consumers—who pay well for their insurance coverage—the care they need to get well. And this does not just happen to alcoholics and addicts; other Americans with different diseases have felt the sting of denial of payment by their insurance companies. Most addicts need three months in treatment to ensure long-term sobriety, but insurance companies usually cover just three to ten days. Then society maligns the addicts for their continued ill behavior. That is like getting half of the chemotherapy needed to treat cancer and yet expecting the cancer to be cured. Consider that when you look at these 2012 figures for some of the top insurance companies and their CEOs.[39]

United Health Care Group
Revenue: $111 billion
CEO compensation: Stephen Hemsley, $34.7 million

WellPoint Inc. Group
Revenue: $61.7 billion
CEO compensation: John Cannon (interim president and CEO for 2012), $6.47 million

Kaiser Foundation Hospitals, Kaiser Foundation Health Plan Inc., and subsidiaries
Revenue: $50.6 billion
CEO compensation: George Halvorson (CEO of Kaiser Permanente), about $7.7 million

Humana Group
Revenue: $37 billion
CEO compensation: Michael B. McCallister, $3.33 million

Aetna
Revenue: $35.54 billion
CEO compensation: Mark T. Bertolini, $4.76 million

Blue Cross Blue Shield
Revenue: $20.9 billion
CEO compensation: Daniel Loepp, $3.8 million

• • •

I received another message, this time on a social networking site.

"Help me," was all it said, along with the woman's name. I contacted her through the same site that she found me on.

Her name was Lauren. She was young, and the family situation she related was beyond imagination in its dysfunction. But as I tell my kids, don't trust everything on the Internet. I went to some lengths to check out her identity and story, mainly though other people on the site whom we both knew.

She was a needle-heroin and smoking-crack addict. And she was sweet and humble and ready to die at her own hand. And I, a stranger, got the SOS distress call and couldn't look away. I was out of favors at many rehab centers—sometimes they are gracious enough to oblige when I ask them to take folks for either full or partial scholarship—so I told Lauren to call every rehab she could find on the Internet. "Start with the ones that are well known and beg," I told her.

And beg she did. The first day, nothing. "Okay," I said, "don't be discouraged."

Lauren lived close to the capital of her state, and the legislature was in session. I did my research and, with the help of a lawyer friend, found out that a bill was up for debate about helping fund private rehabs with state money to increase the bed potential for uninsured alcoholics and addicts. I found out the time and place that the bill would be discussed, was told by the secretary at the statehouse that an open mike would be available for community comments and suggestions, and communicated this to Lauren's mom. "Take her, get her in front on the lawmakers, and have her tell them her story," I said.

The mom was skeptical but followed my advice. She took Lauren to the open meeting on the bill, and Lauren did it! She told the committee of her family's history of substance abuse throughout the generations and how it had devastated her family, robbing it of opportunities such as a college education. She went on to say that health care was rarely offered at the types of jobs her family members were qualified to work at. I gave her support via Bluetooth from my phone, whispering my confidence in her ear and suggesting things for her to say as she shakily stood in front of this imposing committee.

By the end of that day, she was in an excellent rehab. A benefactor had come forward—a woman who sat on the committee donated directly to a rehab for Lauren to obtain quality health care for her disease of addiction. Begging works, folks, and more than that, so can telling your story to people who might have the power to help you when you are injured and have no money. It can't hurt.

Also, almost all rehabs work with companies that lend money specifically for health care needs and offer low rates, many times deferring any payments for many months. This can give the addict time to get back to work.

Finding Recovery without Rehab

I have also seen success with sobriety with no rehab at all. Back when Alcoholics Anonymous (AA) first came on the scene in the mid-1930s, this was the best option for getting sober that alcoholics had. In the 1950s, Narcotics Anonymous, using the same Twelve Steps as AA, began providing support for people whose drug of choice was something other than alcohol, especially heroin and other opiates. Some fundamentalist recovery folks have written about how they believe the Twelve Steps that are the basis of recovery for these peer support groups have been "watered down" by the rehab movement, and that getting back to our roots, working the Steps, getting a sponsor and going to meetings, helping our fellow suffering alcoholics, and doing service work can lead to just as much success as rehab. For some people, this might be true, but as addiction science has progressed so have the approaches to formal treatment, resulting in rehab programs that are very effective in treating addiction, especially for the many addicts who have a co-occurring psychiatric disorder such as depression, anxiety, or PTSD.

So if you have no money and no treatment program is available—or if even if you're already in an outpatient program or have completed an inpatient stay, find a Twelve Step meeting in your community—AA if you're alcoholic or there are no other Twelve Step groups available, or Narcotics Anonymous (NA), Cocaine Anonymous (CA), or another drug-specific, peer-recovery group that will accept opiate addicts—and call someone to take you to a meeting, or just show up and give it a try. You may have to shop around; not every meeting will necessarily be a good fit for you but most people can find a group that meets their needs, where there are people whose stories are similar to theirs and who can provide the ongoing support and motivation that every addict needs for long-term recovery. You should also find a sponsor very soon, someone with at least a couple of years of recovery and of the same sex (opposite if you're gay or lesbian) who can guide you in understanding and applying the Steps. Many people recommend doing ninety meetings in ninety days if you're new to recovery, but you should attend at least two to three meetings a week at first.

Creating a Relapse Prevention Plan

Whether you get treatment and use Twelve Step support, or can only use a Twelve Step or other support program for your recovery management, it's vital—especially with the powerful cravings that opiates can cause—that you have a solid relapse prevention plan in place. This should include

- getting rid of all drugs and paraphernalia, including pill bottles if you used prescription painkillers

- avoiding the people, places, and other triggers you associate with using
- carrying a list with you at all times of people you can call if you do have a craving to use
- keeping a list of Twelve Step meetings handy so you can get to a meeting as soon as possible should a craving strike; having friends and family who can support you when you get into trouble
- taking care of your body—eating healthy foods, getting plenty of sleep, and exercising
- helping someone else in need, either by telling your story at meetings, doing service work, or just volunteering at your favorite nonprofit
- meditating, or praying if you're religious, to manage stress and maintain a sense of gratitude for being drug free

If you should have a slip and use again, don't think it has to turn into a full-blown relapse; get back into your recovery program immediately and remember that you stay clean and sober a day at a time.

• • •

Let me be very frank as someone who is on the front lines, talking with families who need treatment for their loved ones struggling with the disease of addiction. In most cases, it is the old system of haves and have-nots that determines who gets life-saving treatment. And that breaks my heart. It is why I originally went to the media to get help with my addiction. We, a family of four, college educated and insured, could not afford the treatment I needed to get well.

Since the Mental Health Parity and Addiction Equity Act became law in 2008, I have seen some change in the amount of money paid out by insurance companies to treat alcoholism and addiction—but we still have a long way to go. The law "generally" prevents group health plans and health insurance issuers that provide coverage for mental health substance-use-disorders from imposing less-favorable limitations on those benefits than on medical/surgical coverage. What does "generally" mean? I was talking with a neighbor whose husband died of cancer. When he was ill, she even had to fight to get coverage for that disease. Our health care system is broken. Can the government fix it? After reading about all the changes to come, I was left with visions of hoops that will need to be jumped through to get the care you really need and hope that they don't present even more barriers to getting treatment, for both the haves *and* have-nots.

• • •

It was now Christmas Eve, and Tricare had still come up with no real solution for Jeff and his family. So I took to the streets—or, more accurately, to the Internet—and within an hour I had two offers of rehab for this family under extreme stress, a family where the father had fought for our country. It was a Christmas miracle for this very deserving family.

In the next chapter, we will look at special groups—women with children, the elderly, and the emerging autism community as an example of people with co-occurring conditions—and the unique challenges they face in finding the right fit for the rehabilitation they need.

MOMS WITH BABIES
AND OTHER SPECIAL GROUPS

Moms with Babies

"My daughter-in-law is pretty bad off with alcoholism," a colleague who formerly worked at a rehab center told me. "My son and her are really struggling in their relationship, and their baby is just six weeks old. She can be very verbally combative and hard to get along with."

"Great, a hothead," I said to myself. Females with a strong defense mechanism displayed as anger can be hard to deal with. As I've mentioned before, anger is always a secondary emotion. Hiding behind the anger is hurt, fear, or both. Many times, a person who is chronically angry is still reacting to unresolved issues in childhood. I remind myself of this whenever I am confronted with a person who is responding to me with extreme anger. The angrier the person gets, the more nurturing I become, hopefully making him or her feel protected and defusing the misdirected wrath. Having a young infant, I believed, would increase this woman's defense mechanism of anger. I would prove to be right.

"How is the baby?" I asked, trying to assess if she has an infant with any critical problems caused by the mother's alcoholism, such as malnutrition, physical abuse, or fetal alcohol syndrome, a very serious condition of delayed cognitive and social development that may include distinctive malformed facial features.

"The baby is fine," my colleague said. "Maggie managed to not drink while pregnant, as far as I know. I'm her mother-in-law and have worked in the addiction field, but she won't listen to me. Can you please help us do an intervention?"

And I did. As expected, this new young mom was a hothead. First she tried to push us out the front door; then she locked herself in the bathroom with the baby when she realized it was an intervention, with her mother and mother-in-law waiting outside. She was yelling her head off, which frightened the baby, who began to cry. With my encouragement, Maggie calmed herself down for the baby's sake.

I was literally cooing calmness to this mom, with a piece of wood between us. I have done complete interventions this way, with the whole group sitting on the floor outside a locked door, reading their letters of love and wishes. After they have read the letters, I have the family push the letters under the door. Going into this intervention, I knew my biggest barrier to getting this young woman to accept treatment was to find a rehab that accepted moms with babies. It can be done, but not always easily. A website linked to the federal Substance Abuse and Mental Health Services Administration lists 314 substance abuse treatment facilities in the United States that have residential beds for clients' children.[40] The beds are there—you just have to ferret them out. Many list scholarships for indigent moms with babies. If you don't have a computer, remember that public libraries usually do, with free Internet service.

But for now, I was the only one standing at the bathroom door. Maggie was off-the-charts mad at her husband and mother-in-law, so I asked them to give us some space. At the end of this intervention, my colleague, whom I hold in the highest regard, gave me the best compliment: "I understand now what you mean when you say interventions should be all about love."

I eventually found and secured a bed for Maggie and her baby at a wonderful private rehab center on the East Coast. It provided all the services moms needed to feel secure in treatment with their babies. Child care was offered during the day while the women attended their groups. Wonderful play areas, both indoor and outdoor, were available to the little ones. At night, the babies were with their moms, all together in a special building with everything needed to nurture this special population. Sadly, the state funding that allowed this private rehab to offer services to moms and babies was cut not too long ago. But at the moment I was helping Maggie, they were still available to her and her baby. I just had to get her out of the bathroom!

Older Adults

Aging adults with medical conditions in addition to addiction are another special group of addicts. In the middle of the night, sixty-two-year-old Ruth woke up in the worst pain she had ever experienced. She was bent in half, sweating all over, and holding her stomach. She did not understand why she was in so much abdominal pain: she was on a huge amount of opiate pain medication for no reason other than her monstrous addiction. She had fooled her doctors into believing that she was in severe, unrelenting, and pervasive pain from the nebulous diagnosis of fibromyalgia. I am not inferring that fibromyalgia does not exist; it does, and it is a legitimate medical condition. But it is hard to determine if a particular patient really suffers from it. Many addicts look it up online and mimic the symptoms to persuade doctors to prescribe narcotics for them. It is believed that people with fibromyalgia have overactive nerves. This may be responsible for the chronic, all-over pain and tenderness of fibromyalgia. But there is no lab test to confirm a diagnosis of fibromyalgia in patients, according to the Mayo Clinic in Minnesota,[41] so many narcotic addicts use that fact to get prescription drugs.

Ruth had been on large amounts of narcotics for a decade. Constipation is a common side effect of narcotic use, and Ruth had long been experiencing severe, unrelenting bowel issues associated with the constipation while on OxyContin. On this night, she began suffering from extreme pain because of a life-threatening condition: her bowel had ruptured, and toxic fecal matter was leaking all through her abdomen. This had led to an inflammation known as peritonitis and an infection known as sepsis. She woke her husband to tell him how she was feeling, then passed out.

At the hospital, her husband gave his consent for surgeons to perform a high-risk procedure known as a laparotomy to flush out the fecal material and find and repair the tears in his wife's bowels. The surgery did not go well. Ruth had multiple perforations to her bowel due to her chronic constipation, and the sepsis was spreading across her body as the fecal peritonitis traveled throughout her abdomen, affecting most of her internal organs. She was on intensive, multiple antibiotic therapies, given to her through three different intravenous lines. She was unconscious, and pneumonia took over as the sepsis raged up into her lungs. Ruth was in real danger of her body shutting down from multiple organ failure that could end her life.

Again, addiction is a thief. If Ruth had died, her death certificate would have likely read "pervasive peritoneal sepsis due to ruptured bowel" when in reality it should have said "addiction, a brain disorder that alters the mind's ability to control the intake of narcotics." My father's death certificate says "fatal head injury due to automobile accident" when it should say "alcoholism, a brain disease that alters the person's judgment to drive while under the influence of alcohol."

The medical team placed Ruth on a ventilator, and her family—husband, son, parents, and siblings—was told that she would most likely die. The team was preparing the family for the need to stop the ventilator to let Ruth pass on. The family went home to write Ruth letters that would be read to her the next day, before the ventilator that was keeping her alive was turned off.

The family arrived at the hospital the next day and found that the barrage of antibiotics that coursed through Ruth's veins had unexpectedly helped her turn the corner, and she was recovering. Ruth was a strong woman—most addicts and alcoholics are, contrary to what many people believe. We have to be strong to deal and live with this crazy, unrelenting disease.

For the time being, Ruth was out of the woods, but her family was sure she would go back to abusing narcotics when she returned home. She refused to go to addiction rehab following this hospital stay. That's when I got the call. I well understood why the patient needed to go directly from the hospital to rehab. Years ago, I had overdosed on the amphetamine Adderall, which resulted in my hospitalization due to a near heart attack. Within two hours of returning home, I took Adderall again. It makes no sense; addiction is a form of insanity and the brain is just not operating correctly—that's why the Second Step of AA's Twelve Steps says we need to be restored to sanity. There was a good chance that if Ruth went home after being in the hospital, she would return to active addiction. Even though her condition of bowel obstruction and rupture was due to her abuse of opiate pain medication, during her hospital stay she was given opiates to control postoperative pain associated with the intense procedures and operations she endured. The need for opiates for her legitimate pain would continue to tweak the addict brain, and she would be discharged with a persistent craving for opiates. She needed a door-to-door transfer from hospital to rehab. She was just too high-risk to go home.

"Yes, we can do the intervention at the hospital in a conference room," I told Ruth's husband, Bruce, "but I will need to investigate what rehab will take a patient with intense medical issues in combination with her addiction."

When discharged, Ruth would still require medical care. She would have tubes coming from her gallbladder to continue draining fecal material into a separate external bag, be on multiple antibiotics, and have an external colostomy bag to drain feces from her bowel so that the repaired bowel had time to heal. In the future, if enough healthy bowel remained, doctors would reconnect her intestines, and the colostomy bag outside her abdomen would no longer be needed. The gallbladder bag would need to be removed in two weeks.

The first rehab I investigated originally said yes to Ruth's admission, but in the hospital parking lot, while I was on my way to do the intervention, I got a call. "The team has re-evaluated your patient, and we have decided to decline her admission." Shit! The conversation went downhill from there. I can't express in writing how angry I was. No point.

So with the family and the medical team assembling for the intervention, I had nowhere to send the patient. Back on the phone, the next rehab asked, "Is she able to ambulate and do her ADLs"—activities of daily living, such as bathing and brushing her teeth. "Pretty sure," I replied, "but let me check."

Now I went undercover. I handed my Chihuahua, Lucy, to a family member and said I would be right back. Going to the patients' nurses' station, I put on a paper gown and went into her room.

"Hi," I said to Ruth as I entered.

"Hi," she replied. She looked pretty good sitting up in bed, but I needed to see her get around. "Are you able to get out of bed and pick up your slippers off the floor?" I asked.

She looked at me as if to say, "Can't you do it? You're right there," but she obliged me. I stayed close in case this was too tough an assignment for her. But she got right up, walked over to the slippers, bent over, and moved them with no problem.

Next I went to the bathroom.

"Do you think you can clean the sink area of your stuff on your own?" As a second thought I added, "Maybe brush your teeth, then clean up after yourself?"

She looked at me oddly, but maybe she was thinking that this was a test nurses gave to all patients. I hoped so anyway. This time she grabbed her walker, but she moved very steadily with it. She got to the bathroom, let the walker go, and did her morning routine with no problems.

"Can I hand you a new colostomy bag? You can change it while you are in there."

"Sure," she said.

I peeked in to see if she needed anything and saw her expertly changing her colostomy bag with the supplies I handed her. Yes! I could give the new rehab a good report. I left the room and never explained what this was about. She must have thought I was nutty—which is what the profession of intervention is like a lot of the time.

As the family was assembling in the conference room for the intervention, I got confirmation from the rehab that it would take Ruth after hearing my report on her condition. At times it helps to be a nurse who does interventions.

The family was ready for the intervention. With my direction, they had decided to read the letters to Ruth that they had prepared before they were going to turn off her ventilator and let her pass away. I often say my interventions are like a eulogy. How often does a group of people surround you and tell you how much they care about you and what they find special about you while you are alive? Hardly ever. A few staff members who had never been involved in an intervention also attended, with the family's permission.

After everyone was settled into the conference area, I walked back into Ruth's room with Lucy in my arms. "Hey, Ruth. My name is Joani, and there are a few folks who really love you who are waiting to see you," I said. "You just have to follow me and my dog Lucy and absorb all the love."

Ruth looked at me completely deadpan and said, "I thought you were one of the regular nurses."

"I have lots of jobs around here," I replied.

"Okay, I guess," she said, as she commenced to put her slippers on and follow the yellow brick road—that is, the tile leading from the nurses' station. Slippers, little dog—I got a weird *Wizard of Oz* feeling. "If I only had a brain" was going through my head. "If I only had a brain that worked right" was my next thought; then those lovely poppy fields were dancing in my brain and I was way off track. "Okay, Joani," I said to myself, "get yourself back in the game."

Ruth's large family was standing to greet us, and one by one they gave her emaciated frame a gentle but firm hug.

"Please, Ruth, sit next to your son," I said, "And I will explain who I am and why we are here."

She was compliant and sat down. I threw Lucy gently into her lap.

"Hey, little guy," she said. Poor Lucy—everyone thinks she is a boy, although she does not seem to mind. As long as you pet her and give her love and warmth, she is happy to be in your presence.

"Ruth, I am not one of the floor nurses. I am sorry about the charade, but it was necessary, and I will explain later."

She again looked at me deadpan. She had been through a lot. She was responding to Lucy and petting her.

"All these people here love you, and they were so afraid for your life this past week. You know your bowel ruptured due to the chronic constipation brought on by narcotic dependence, correct?"

"Yes," she said, quietly.

"Well, today is your lucky day. All these folks want to share their love with you, and they have a plan that will help you with your addiction."

She just looked at me, blinking soft blue eyes.

"Ruth, I know your pain. I am an addict and alcoholic who got better through an intervention that was done with me when my youngest was in diapers. I have sat in your seat."

She smiled at me weakly. A good sign, I thought.

The group then went around and read their letters as I called on them. A box of Kleenex made a few rounds around the room. Interestingly, Lucy sensed that someone in the room other than Ruth needed her comfort. Ruth's son, Josh, just out of his teens, was crying uncontrollably as each letter was read. Lucy softly left Ruth's lap and crawled into Josh's lap and up his chest and gave him a lick. She then sat right between Ruth and Josh. For the rest of the intervention, mother and son connected while both petted Lucy, their hands periodically touching over Lucy's back. (After the intervention, the hospital's psychologist, who had never sat in on an intervention until this one, came up to me and said, "That dog is a miracle.")

Ruth readily agreed to go to treatment. She nodded her head, and I asked, "Are you saying 'yes' to rehab?"

She nodded her head again.

"Let me hear it, girl, loud and clear!"

"Yes to rehab!" she yelled, and I led the group in a big round of applause and fresh tears as her son held her tight. One week later, an employee from the treatment center that had turned down Ruth's case was at a professional workshop at the rehab where Ruth was ultimately admitted. The employee later called me and said, "I saw the woman we turned down. She almost ran me down with her walker in the cafeteria." I laughed. "Talk to your team," I said. "Tell them to trust me. As a nurse for many years, when I say a patient is not over the top medically, I mean it."

But sometimes patients are burdened with heavy medical problems in addition to addiction, and where do they go? At the end of this book, I will list rehab facilities that take the more medically complicated patients. Treatment centers that accommodate patients with addiction and other medical concerns come at a cost, though ironically, the more physical problems a patient has, the better most health insurance plans cover the stay.

· · ·

Maggie was still in the bathroom with her baby, but she was quiet. I was telling her my story of addiction and how my husband potty trained our son while I was at rehab. (I am still not sure whether I am happy about this or I feel guilty about it. The reality is probably closer to feeling regret—regret that I missed the experience. Addiction *is* a thief.)

"Maggie, I had to leave my babies at home, and that almost broke my heart, but we have found a rehab where you can take your baby with you! She will sleep in a crib in your room at night. They will bring her to you during the day when she needs to breast-feed. They have wonderful staff to watch over her while you are in group or classes."

Nothing. But she was not yelling. Sometimes my instincts tell me to shut up, and this was one of those times. I waited quietly until I couldn't take it anymore.

"How much did Valarie weigh when she was born?" I asked. It was on the neutral subject of babies that she and I bonded. Swapping everyday mom/baby stories through a closed door, she started to trust me. Then, finally, she got to the heart of it.

"Joani, I can go to treatment with you, but I cannot stomach sitting around with my mother-in-law listening to letters. Can we just go?"

This was music to my ears. "Yep. Better yet, why don't I get everyone out of the house as we pack? I will have them wait at the end of the driveway to wave good-bye, so they are not too hurt. Is that okay?"

She agreed. "Tell me when they are gone and I will come out."

I went back to the living room. "Hey, guys, good news. She says she will go to treatment, but she wants everyone out of the house and will not listen to the letters. Don't worry, I will give the letters to her therapist, and if she can handle it, they will go over them with her at the treatment facility."

Every daughter/mother-in-law relationship in America seems to be laden with issues. But when your mother-in-law is a big dog in recovery at a rehab center and is sober, and her son, your husband, is sober, it is tough to hear them without feeling they are being "holier than thou." That, and her husband

and his family come from a different socioeconomic class than Maggie's family. I think Maggie's defense mechanisms stemmed in part from her family's economical and educational differences. In truth, I know that her mother-in-law loved her and the baby, but Maggie had her back up.

When everyone had left the house, I gave Maggie the all clear. Babe in arms, she came out of the bathroom and we started the process of packing for two, mom and baby. It was a privilege for me to help her with this task, and after working as an RN in the newborn nursery so many years, I felt comfortable with a baby in my arms, and I realized how much I missed it. I changed the baby's diaper as Maggie gathered her things.

Once we had settled into the car, we were off. As promised, the intervention "team" waited at the end of the driveway and waved us on. Maggie did wave back. And three years later, she is still sober.

The rehab facility Maggie went to no longer takes moms and babies, but a few treatment centers I have worked with since then do, and they do a great job. One is state run, one is private, and a third is an extended-care facility.

People with Developmental Disabilities

Recently, I have encountered more and more members of another special group of addicts who need attention: people with developmental disorders. Rehab centers need to start developing programs for this emerging population. One of the most neglected of these populations are people with autism.

"Beyond our son Steve's addiction to opiate pain meds, he has always struggled and has been different," said Susan, a flight attendant of many years. She had told me she needed to speak with me in private, without the rest of the people participating in the intervention listening in. This request has only been made to me a few times, but I always respect what the family needs prior to the intervention. This is where I get the information I need to do the best job possible.

"Tell me, how?" I asked, simply.

"Well, school was tough. He was diagnosed with ADHD. He had a hard time understanding what was taught to him, although he is a bright kid."

Because I have two kids on the autism spectrum, my internal flag was starting to go up. "Tell me about his friendships growing up."

"He did not have many friends. He was socially awkward."

"In what way?" I prompted her.

"Well, it is hard to put your finger on it, but he just did not pick up on social cues and turned a lot of kids off. You know, talking about things off topic, or he would repeat the same phrase over and over." Repeating words or phrases is common with verbal children who have autism; it's called "echolalia."

"What about sensory issues," I asked. "Was he sensitive to noise or touch or smell?"

"Oh my God," she said. "You could not chew gum around him. It drove him nuts. And in the movies, he always covered his ears. The movie was always too loud."

Lately, this situation has happened to me with alarming frequency. When talking to parents about their adult children who need treatment for substance use disorder, I suspect their kids have undiagnosed autism. Autism now affects 1 in 88 people, 1 in 54 boys, according to Autism Speaks, a well-respected organization for support and research for autism spectrum disorders.[42] This population is getting older, and I believe that just as rehabs have begun to recognize the prevalence of other psychiatric disorders among addicts and the need to address them and the addiction simultaneously, they will soon need to start special programs for people on the autism spectrum. Every psychiatric disorder presents unique treatment challenges and the autism spectrum is no exception. People with this disorder have learning needs that are unique, especially because of their difficulty with auditory comprehension and their inability to handle large crowds of people due to sensory-overload propensities.

I asked Susan very gently if anyone had ever suggested that her son might be on the autism spectrum. "Yes," she said. "I have had some professionals suggest that Steve has Asperger's." Asperger's syndrome is considered to be an autism spectrum disorder and is marked by difficulties in social interaction and nonverbal communication. People with Asperger's are known to have repetitive patterns of behavior and intense, obsessive interest in specific areas. Anxiety disorders are almost always associated with Asperger's. What sets Asperger's apart from other types of autism is its relative preservation of linguistic and cognitive development. Asperger's syndrome is no longer listed separately in the *Diagnostic and Statistical Manual of Mental Disorders* but is now grouped with the diagnosis "high-functioning autism."[43]

I wondered why the family had not followed through with confirming this possible diagnosis. We know that the earlier someone is diagnosed with a developmental disorder, the more likely that person will be to lead a positive, functional life. But with Steve, that ship had sailed, and we needed to look at what could be done now to help him.

"Susan, I think that could be a correct diagnosis from what you have told me," I said, adding that I have two kids on the autism spectrum. "I think the rehab you have picked out for him is too big. With over a hundred patients at a time in classes and the cafeteria, he will be sensory overloaded. More than likely his anxiety will be very high, and he will have a hard time concentrating on the program."

A specialist in autism at the Johns Hopkins Center for Autism and Developmental Disorders, where my kids were diagnosed, described my son's autism to me in a way I could relate to. "Just think if someone plunked you down in France and you don't speak French. That is how a person with autism feels." Their auditory comprehension with language is very weak. To compensate for this deficit, they become visual learners; the environment around them becomes very important. So when the environment changes, or even if plans change, they can get very unsettled. In their mind they have visualized what is to happen.

This knowledge is a tremendous help to me when I am doing an intervention with someone who has autism. I know going into the intervention that the person will need a brochure from the rehab facility with lots of pictures and a few days to plan the trip to rehab. The patient's need for control, due to insecurities over what is perceived to be an unpredictable environment, means he or she will need to plan the trip, and I accommodate this need by suggesting it from the get-go. I give the patient control, ask what day works best to go to rehab, and say I will return to pick him or her up.

In Steve's case, we picked out a much smaller rehab than the one his mother had chosen, one with just twelve beds. I told the staff about his suspected autism diagnosis. On staff at this rehab was a therapist who specialized in developmental disabilities. But again, the rehab came at a cost. I suggested that Susan look around for grants for people with disabilities. They are there, but you have to do your research and be persistent.

Steve was so sweet. He called me the day before the planned trip.

"Joani, do you mind if I have my dad drive me to rehab?"

Again, he was responding to his inner needs. When his environment is not predictable or as understandable to him as it might be for the average person, his dad represents continuity. I understood this and did not take it personally. I am always thrilled when my patients make it to rehab any way they can.

"Not at all, Steve. Will you find me on Facebook or email me to let me know how you are doing?"

"You bet," he said, and then paused. I have learned with my kids to wait a second as they formulate their words. "Thank you for your help."

"My privilege, Steve."

My hope is that rehabs around the country will see this emerging need in the autism population along with other developmental disabilities—as they've begun to do with severe mental illness—and provide programs to help. Colleges around the country are creating programs for members of the high-functioning autism community and sober dorms just for recovering students. Times are a-changing!

• • •

With the population aging, there's a growing number of people who suffer from chronic pain and addiction, especially to opiate painkillers. In the next chapter, we will look at how these and other chronic pain victims can be helped.

THE PAIN GAME

Real or Not?

It is often hard to tell when a person who has become addicted to opiate painkillers prescribed for chronic pain really is hurting bad enough to need them. Like most things with addicts, the truth lies in the middle, at least in the beginning.

I've talked about how addiction is the perfect storm of three factors: genetics, psychological influences, and social influences. When these three ingredients collide, addiction flares up like a flash fire that goes on to engulf a person's life. Here's a bit more of my personal story as a case in point.

I had been alcohol-free for six years. I had gone to a psychiatrist, Dr. James Kehler, for chronic anxiety and depression, and he suggested I give up drinking. I was in my twenties, and my drinking was escalating, resulting in insomnia, shaky hands in the morning, and bone-numbing hangovers, complete with crushing anxiety and depression with thoughts of suicide. Dr. Kehler did not come out and call me an alcoholic. I don't know if this was a deliberate part of his strategy but I do know that I gave up alcohol and was put on the antidepressant doxepin (Sinequan), a tricyclic antidepressant medication that became instrumental in my life in ways I never expected.

As I shared earlier, both of my parents were alcoholics and addicts, and my dad was dead by this point in my life, dying at the age of forty-seven in a car accident caused by his driving his beloved Mustang while drunk. It would have been his fourth DUI that year. Being a big dog in the legal world, he never suffered official consequences from his DUIs. My mom's death would follow. She was addicted to tranquilizers and previously dependent on cigarettes and beer, which she gave up when she became ill with chronic obstructive pulmonary disease. She could not smoke anymore, nor drink beer. The beer extended her stomach, further compromising her already comprised lungs and making it even more difficult for her to breathe. So, as I mentioned earlier, I already had one of the major factors for addiction going for me: genetics, which accounts for 40 to 60 percent of a person's propensity to be afflicted with the disease.

Those blessed six years when I was alcohol-free were some of the best years of my life. I was active with work and friends, dating, traveling, buying my first home, gardening, attending the theater and independent films, and working as an RN in a newborn nursery and neonatal critical care unit.

And then the newer antidepressants came out—the selective serotonin reuptake inhibitors, or SSRIs. The pioneer was Prozac. Tricyclic drugs like the doxepin that I was on work by elevating norepinephrine and serotonin levels in the brain, but they also interfere with a range of other neurotransmitter systems and this leads to numerous, potentially serious side effects. The newer SSRIs not only could get the job done—increasing serotonin in the brain by blocking its reuptake at the cell receptor site—but the big news was that patients suffered far fewer side effects because the SSRI were selective—honing in on the serotonin and its receptor site, and not interacting with other brain functions.

So Dr. Kehler decided to switch me to this new medication. I felt great on Prozac; the side effects I had experienced with doxepin—shaky hands, dry mouth, the need to urinate frequently, and requiring at least nine hours of sleep a night—abated. I slept great, and I was energized and interested in a variety of activities and hobbies. It was difficult at first to achieve orgasm while on Prozac, but with time and creativity, that was no deterrent.

However, very subtly, my lower back started to ache. I remember the day clearly when I realized there might be a problem. I was standing in my nursing clogs, leaning against a counter where the baby formula was stored in the nursery. I was talking with a fellow RN.

"I don't know what's up," I said, "but my lower back is bugging me a lot." I was working three units: the newborn nursery, neonatal intensive care, and also picking up the odd shift on ambulatory surgery. Fast forward a year, and I had suffered a legitimate back injury on the job while transporting a heavy patient who was having a heart attack. Two years later, after suffering from chronic pain and now addicted to narcotics, I had a spinal fusion.

The surgeons who did my fusion told me that my back had been fractured at some point in my life. I was unaware this had occurred, but apparently it happens frequently to little kids. They fall off swings or the bottoms of slides and fracture the lower part of their spine called the L5, S1, which stands for the fifth vertebra in the lumbar region of the back and the first vertebra of the sacrum area of the back. These vertebrae are at the lowest point of the spinal column. The doxepin had been relieving both my depression and the pain from my original back injury through its activity with neural pathways, and I was unaware of this. I know now that when I was taken off doxepin and placed on Prozac, I started to feel the pain of the original injury to my back.

After the injury at work that exacerbated by back problems, I tried numerous other treatments to alleviate my pain: steroid shots, acupuncture, and physical therapy. For two years I stayed away from opiate medications. I knew from my drinking days that they were dangerous for me to take. I eventually had an MRI of my back and then was sent to a surgical team. Being in the health field, I found the best doctors available. I remember asking the orthopedic surgeon whether, if he had my back, he would he go under the knife to have a spinal fusion. He replied, "If I could stay on the anti-inflammatory medications to relieve the pain, no, I would not have it." Since then, and even after the back accident at work, I have often thought that if I had gone back on doxepin, I could have avoided surgery and ten years of hell on narcotics. Hindsight is truly 20/20.

So one day, while still investigating other treatments for my pain prior to surgery, I took two of my soon-to-be fiancé's Percocet, an opiate narcotic he had for recurring kidney stone pain. I knew the pills were in my house, and they spoke to me often, whispering their twisted love song to me from way back in the medicine cabinet. The combination of the constant malicious song and my unremitting pain led me to open that deadly bottle of narcotics.

Upon swallowing them, I was almost immediately aware of a sense of euphoria. The sun came out, I felt confident and comfortable in my formally insecure skin, *and my pain was gone.* The love affair began—as did my almost deadly obsession with opiate pain medication.

Following surgery, a new MRI revealed the train wreck that my back had become, with twelve pieces of titanium now holding my spine together. At this point, the pain game started in earnest. No one could say the surgery was a success or a failure. Pain is subjective, and so I was able to obtain a huge amount of medication to counter it. I also used other physical problems as excuses to obtain opiates. My opiate habit steadily increased through the phenomenon of tolerance—an addict will always need more of the drug to achieve the same effect; this continues until the last deadly dose is consumed. I was learning that addiction is a chronic, progressive, and fatal disease.

Father Martin, of Father Martin's Ashley treatment program, was famous for saying that for the person afflicted with the disease of chemical dependency, "One drug/drink is too many, and a thousand is never enough." That is a core truth for every addict/alcoholic.

A short digression: Recently I was weaving honeysuckle vines into the lattice wall in my garden. I was in a hurry and stood on the planter below the honeysuckle, maybe three feet high. Rather than wearing safe, flexible gardening shoes, I was in fancy, sexy wedge heels, complete with peep toes for my manicured feet. I fell backward off of the planter. The fall seemed to take a long time, but my life did not pass before my eyes—my addiction did. My prayer on the way down was just, "Help me, God." My biggest fear was reinjuring my back. I felt that God was near, and the only consequence from the fall was that I bit my tongue when my head hit my stucco house.

Back to my pain game: my doctor shopping was now a full-time job as I continually pursued the narcotics that my body demanded more and more of. From unnecessary root canals to a temporomandibular joint workup for my popping jaw, my knowledge as a nurse helped me to devise the deceptions needed to obtain narcotics for medical conditions I did not have. My surgeons finally called me on it and sent me to the Johns Hopkins pain management department. I was fully prepared to pump them for even more opiate narcotics, and they were fully prepared to *not* give me narcotics. Damn it. Apparently somebody had clued them in. "What you need to do," one of the doctors advised, "is to take an alternative medication to narcotics for your pain, the drug doxepin, a tricyclic antidepressant that works on the neural pathways in the brain and can work very well for pain. You will need to take a minimum of 150 milligrams."

I sat there, staring at my doctors. "Well I'll be," I thought. I had been on doxepin for ten years. Then I started to put the pieces together. My back pain started when I was taken off doxepin and put on Prozac.

But I was not done with whining for narcotics. Like a toddler breaking down a parent for a forbidden extra cookie, a narcotic addict can hammer away at a doctor like no one else, and I left Hopkins with both doxepin *and* narcotics. I started taking the doxepin again, but the narcotic game still moved full speed ahead as I employed numerous creative skills to obtain the narcotics I needed.

Then something happened. I met Dr. Phil McGraw through an almost chance encounter that fell from the sky into my lap. I was not looking for help for myself. I wanted advice from Dr. Phil about my son, Max, who at the tender age of two years was showing developmental symptoms not normal for his age. Dr. Phil, knowing of my addiction, which I readily admitted, wanted to talk to me and my husband about my addiction in a private studio in Los Angeles, and to show a tape of that discussion on his prime time yearly special. We agreed.

Dr. Phil hit me over the head with a two-by-four after I refused treatment, something I'll be forever grateful for. He said my son's eventual help will never be very effective unless I get well first. He also pointed out that the very custody of my kids was in jeopardy, my profession was in jeopardy, and my life itself was in dire peril. What I heard the most was that I could lose my children, either through the law or by dying. I could handle dying if it was just me. I had struggled through many things—my parents' early deaths, molestation, and my unremitting addiction. Life had been hard, but I did not want those precious babies to be without a mom. So I went to treatment for three months and turned my life around. I now joke with friends, "Yep, I stayed on my post-op pain meds for ten years," adding, "If I need another surgery, please tell my doctors to send me *directly* to rehab following the procedure and please come visit me on Sundays!"

Back home, the doxepin worked wonders on my residual back pain. Spinal fusions statistically take care of about 70 percent of a patient's back pain, and so it was with me. Also, a few Tylenol will take the edge off. I used to think Tylenol was a crap drug, but when the available options of pain management drugs become limited, it is amazing what regular medications can do! I also take anti-inflammatory medications like Advil at times. It works great but bothers my stomach. Aleve, which is longer acting, will bother the stomach less but is not as powerful as Advil.

My pain doctor and I had a frank conversation about my addiction after I came home from rehab. I told her I could not take narcotics safely, that I was an addict. And something amazing happened! She is the only doctor I have been honest with who did not respond by "firing" me from her practice because I conned her for narcotics. She was empathetic and thanked me for telling her the truth. Then she went a step further. "We will find alternative ways to deal with your pain," she told me, as she hugged me. She understood. She understood that addiction is a medical condition, not a moral problem or a failure of will. I will always be grateful to her.

Twice I have needed more intensive therapy for unremitting pain, most recently about seven years ago. My doctor had me sedated and injected my right hip area with a combination of glucose and steroids. "But no light sedation party for you," she said, not unkindly, before introducing me to her anaesthesiologist. "This is the patient, Joani, I was telling you about," she said to the anaesthesiologist. "She has a strong history of the illness of addiction." Wow, I said to myself, "the illness of addiction." Not "a junkie," "lowlife," "degenerate," "deadbeat," or "scum of the earth."

"Nice to meet you," the anaesthesiologist said. "What I do with my patients with a history of addiction is take you under pretty deeply, so you do not experience a twilight effect of light sedation. I don't use any medications with opiates in them. Then I bring you back up to consciousness quickly so again, no grogginess. We find this helps to not tweak the addict brain into craving after anaesthesia." I did not know if I was happy about this. I was kind of looking forward to "light sedation," but on the other hand, I was glad I had a pain doctor who understood my unique challenges when it came to procedures that were dangerous for me because of my addiction.

Alternatives to Abusing Painkillers

Although different organizations offer numerous recommendations on ways to treat pain and addiction, many of these suggestions are not very helpful because they are time consuming. Addicts need to take a lot of time in exploring alternative ways to treat their pain and medical conditions, and managed care gives doctors very little time. So what sounds good in theory is many times hard to pull off in reality. You, the addict, have to be your own advocate, and I know this is hard if you are not in the frame of mind to stay clean. You need a doctor to help you, but we are so hard to read and so good at what we do— feigning pain and illness. It is a complicated issue.

For example, according to a study of pain management by the National Institute on Drug Abuse (NIDA) released in October 2011, roughly 116 million people in the United States have chronic pain, but no one knows how many of those people are addicts using the legal system to feed their addictions. The NIDA study reported, "Estimates of addiction among chronic pain patients vary widely, from 3 to 40 percent. This variability is the result of differences in treatment duration, insufficient research on long-term outcomes, and disparate study populations and measures used to assess abuse or addiction."[44] I conducted my own unofficial research by sitting in dozens of pain management waiting rooms during my days of active addiction. I chatted with lots of folks and traded tricks with some of the people I met on what to say to improve my odds of procuring the narcotic I was after. One addict can measure up another addict pretty quickly, and those waiting rooms are habituated by a lot of addicts.

The NIDA study on pain management goes on to say that it is imperative to take a long history from a patient, looking for a personal or family history of drug abuse or mental illness. I almost laughed when I read that. What addict going to a doctor's office looking for narcotics is going to tell the doc his good old dad is a crack addict or his sister shoots dope? There is a wide divide between theory and reality, but we must keep trying.

I think this theory is far easier to put into practice: monitor the patient for drug-seeking behaviors. A patient with an addiction will make up excuses, like saying he lost his prescription, or the whole bottle he had fell into a toilet. Today, many doctors who prescribe opiates will accept this sort of excuse from a patient only one time. Also, many doctors require their patients who are on opiates to sign contracts stating they will receive their medication only from them and use only one pharmacy. This is easy to get around if you don't use insurance, although some pharmacies no longer accept scripts for opiates that do not go through insurance. I understand that in theory this can slow down doctor shopping from the pharmacies, but what about the legitimate person in pain with no insurance? The contracts that doctors ask patients to sign do protect the physicians if the patients obtain a prescription from another doctor and then the patient dies of an overdose.

I am a successfully recovering chronic pain patient with addiction, and according to the studies, I am doing or have done everything the reports suggest an addict with pain should do. I know I am just one person, but for me the suggestions below have worked. Having said that, I do believe there is a group of people who will never get their real pain alleviated without opiates, and I will explore that further in the next chapter. But here are the things research suggests people with chronic pain look into:

1. Alternative medication for pain, such as antidepressants.
2. Regional anaesthetic interventions (like the steroid-glucose block I had injected under anaesthesia).
3. Surgery. I was relieved of 70 percent of my pain, the most you can reasonably expect from back surgery, through a spinal fusion.
4. Psychological therapies. I have a psychiatrist and attend recovery meetings.
5. Rehabilitative/physical therapy. Almost daily, I do stretches that I learned in physical therapy.

6. Complementary and alternative medicine. I get regular massage from an experienced therapist who has a strong background in working with back issues. Acupuncture has proven effective for treating chronic pain caused by a variety of conditions.

I will tell you what impedes an addict from getting well under our health care system. As a seasoned opiate drug addict, I have found that once health care providers discover I am a drug addict, they drop me from their practices. I need help. And I do have pain.

I don't think other patients with health conditions get "fired" by their doctors. A far more therapeutic response to that patient would be, "I understand now that you are having problems with addiction. What can I do to *help* you?" I think that at various times in my life, a gentle hand on my shoulder or an understanding ear could have made a huge difference in the outcome of my health. Being treated like a "bad person" instead of a "sick person" for having the disease of addiction perpetuates the shame and drives the addict deeper into illness. Remember, there is a psychological aspect to the perfect storm of addiction. To feel psychologically like shit because you have this quirky brain disease makes you feel horrible about yourself for the things you have done to obtain opiates, and you then seek to numb yourself out further.

My call to doctors and other health care workers is to try compassion, and be professional and help addicts find the resources they need to get well. Consider this: if your patient had breast cancer, to whom would you refer that patient? You would not just lecture and demean the patient for having the disease of cancer. And please don't fire the chronic pain sufferer (real or not) who is discovered to be an addict. *Do no harm.* By treating us as "bad people" you are hurting us "sick people" who need your help.

I'd like to end this chapter by discussing two points:

- The backlash from doctors' overprescribing opiates and addicts' abusing the system has hurt those who legitimately need these very useful medications.
- I did my own unofficial research to see how easy it is to obtain narcotics, even for me, a well-known, self-admitted addict. As a result, I want to point out to doctors one small change they can make in their offices that will help both the health care worker and the addict stay honest.

Overreaction to Painkiller Abuse

The backlash can be extreme, as doctors are increasingly under the gun to rein in overprescribing opiates by the U.S. Drug Enforcement Agency and other entities. My aunt is in her eighties. Though she walks with a cane and had two open-heart surgeries in 2012, she is still active. I love her dearly; she is the one who made the summers in my youth wonderful, loving, and, most important, normal. She has never had an issue with addiction or alcoholism. In 2013, she tore her rotator cuff quite badly, and it caused her much physical pain. She is not a good surgical candidate due to her heart issues. Her general doctor had been prescribing the lowest dose possible of Vicodin, and it was working, so she never requested an increase in dosage or the amount of pills prescribed.

Then one day, her doctor told her she would have to go to a pain management doctor to get her medication. This doctor had known my aunt for years, but now she had to go to a clinic every month with her cane, pee into a cup, and sign a contract to get her pain medication. She told me, "Joani, they treat me like a drug addict." Before, her doctor could just call in her prescription, but now she had to make a monthly driving trip to see the doctor. This is a blatant case of having gone too far with the fear of overprescribing opiates and the consequences the doctors are starting to feel. On one hand, this is a good thing in recognizing the abuse of opiate painkillers, but we must use common sense when changing how opiates are prescribed.

Easy Access to Opiate Painkillers

I did an experiment to show how easy it is to still get opiates from doctors. I went to four doctors in one week. The first was my long-standing primary care physician. I had gotten a flyer in the mail about a new physician in the practice. She was young and had a foreign-sounding name—ripe pickings for this addict. Also, the newest doctor in a practice is the least booked and, therefore, the easiest to get to see. That can be used as an excuse as to why you are not seeing your usual physician. I also know my regular MD's day off, so I made sure to go in on that day so as to not run into her. My primary care doctor knows all about my addiction illness, struggles, and ultimate recovery, and it is in my electronic chart for all to see. This new doctor would have access to my history in the computer record, but under managed care, she would be under pressure to see many patients in one day.

Managed care, as I have written and I strongly believe, is the most important variable that has been responsible for the explosion of prescription drug dependence. A close second to managed care, I believe, are the greedy pharmaceutical companies, with their well-documented campaigns of giving out misleading information about their addictive medications and, like many drug pushers, giving you a taste of their product through free samples distributed to doctors' offices.

So I went to doctor number 1. She was sweet but not completely secure being a new doctor not in her native country.

My appointment was for back pain. I talked her up about her home country and how she got here, basically distracting her. I then told her I was traveling a lot and my back was acting up. She did a quick evaluation of my reflexes and range of motion, which I faked. I then told her I needed a prescription for an opiate pain medication, just to use occasionally when I travel. I added that Tylenol was not working and that I was suffering from a persistent hiatal hernia from having had a breech, nine-pound, ten-ounce baby at age forty-four.

Bingo!—out came the script pad, and I skipped out the door with my opiates.

I have a simple but life-saving tip for those who work in doctors' offices. Before prescribing any medication, health care workers will ask patients if they are allergic to any medications and check the red box at the top of the electronic chart where allergies are listed. It is the number one rule in nursing and medical schools to check for patient allergies. My suggestion is this: when a patient in a health care practice is a known addict, put that information in the red box and indicate that he is allergic to all mood-altering drugs! It will work, and it is so simple.

Doctor number 2 was a new internist. I asked my gynecologist if he could suggest a good internist. He did, and I made an appointment. I flattered him by telling him what a wonderful recommendation he got from my gynecologist. I told him I am changing from my family practice doctor because I wanted a more comprehensive health evaluation. He agreed and did a physical. He could see the scar on my back and hip from my spinal fusion, and we talked about that and the continued pain that was controlled well with opiates. I had previously filled out my history on a secure online form to save managed care some time.

The doctor looked over my medication history. "Are these medications still working well for you?"

"Yes," I said. Out came the prescription pad, and out the door I went with opiate pain medication.

Doctor number 3 was at my old haunt, the local urgent care center, or "doc-in-a-box," a nickname that comes from the drive-in quality of this sort of practice where no appointment is needed. I would go to this doctor every time I got a cold, and he would give me Tussionex HC, a cough syrup with hydrocodone in it. Now it was eight years later, and this same doctor did not seem to remember me. I told him I was going to California on a nonstop flight and that with my spinal fusion, my back could really bother me on long flights and I needed an opiate medication for the trip.

"Why did you not go to your regular doctor?" he asked.

"I just forgot until it got too late to get an appointment." Forgetting makes it seem like the opiate medication is not that important.

Okay, he said, and out came the prescription pad. Before giving me the script, he made me give a urine sample to be sent out to check for controlled drugs in my system. I obliged willingly, knowing I had no drugs in my system. If my urine came back positive for opiates, he would know I had been doctor shopping if I started hitting his clinic on a frequent basis. But I did ask him why I needed to leave a urine specimen.

"The DEA is coming down hard on doctors prescribing narcotics, so we have to keep records."

Good, I thought, until I remembered my eighty-two-year-old aunt and the requirements imposed on her to receive her low-dose narcotic.

Incidentally, I paid a heavy cash price for that urine test, which the staff told me insurance would not cover. I had to pay the cash before I got the prescription for the opiates. A small voice in my head told me something was not quite right with

that. Was someone padding the account for the patient re-
questing opiates? My instincts are usually right.

Doctor number 4 was at another urgent care center, but this
doctor knew me well. I tell him my back was bothering me and
asked if he could prescribe an opiate for me.

"Joani," he said, "I am not even going to charge you for this
visit. It would be considered malpractice for me to prescribe a
controlled substance to a known drug addict."

Yes, he got it right, and he got it wrong. He was nice and re-
spectful, but he did not take the time to ask me if I was having
a problem again with addiction. If I had any other disease that
was considered chronic, progressive, and fatal, would he not
explore the possibility of a recurrence and talk with me about
that? Addiction does not get the respect it deserves. I know addicts are tough patients, but we did not choose this disease.
Help us; don't shame us or ignore us. We are complicated and,
yes, time consuming. If you save one person, you save the entire world, so do no harm for this one patient on this one day,
and take the extra time, please.

• • •

In the next chapter, we will look at some of the new theories on
addiction and controversial treatments that are being imple-
mented when treating addicts. Are they working?

9

ALTERNATIVE TREATMENTS FOR OPIATE ADDICTION

"I didn't have the balls to tell you that I started taking Suboxone last March," Lisa spit at me, as she sat crossed-legged on the floor rolling tip money from her part-time waitressing job into coin wrappers. She was my live-in nanny, friend, fellow addict, my unofficial adopted daughter, and my heart.

We were fighting, something that rarely happened with us, but when people live together, conflicts inevitably arise, and we were in the middle of one. This fight wasn't about anything big enough to mention, but Lisa must have wanted to tell me about the Suboxone because, in the heat of an argument that had nothing to do with drugs, she spilled it out like a dirty little secret. It should not be a dirty little secret.

Medications Used to Treat Opiate Addiction

The three FDA-approved anti-craving medications for alcohol dependence are disulfiram, acamprosate, and naltrexone (Vivitrol). There are also three FDA-approved medications for opiate dependence: methadone, buprenorphine, and naltrexone. Buprenorphine is now the primary medication used in rehabs around the country for detoxing opiate-dependent patients. It is also used for treatment of patients who are chronic addicts and cannot maintain sobriety off of opiates. Lisa knew about my experiences with buprenorphine, the synthetic opioid component of Suboxone, and she had sensed that I would disagree with her decision to take this medication. But with all the new research citing low sobriety statistics for opiate addicts, I—all of us in the field—have to think outside the box when it comes to this persistent, pervasive, and devastating disease.

Buprenorphine and Methadone

"I was either going to shoot dope [heroin] or get on Suboxone," Lisa said. This young woman has undergone perhaps $250,000 worth of excellent treatment and had been very active in the recovery community. She did trauma work at a wonderful inpatient rehab around her intense childhood trauma issues, and yet she was still craving opiates and was so afraid of relapsing again. How could I argue with her decision?

Suboxone is a combination of two drugs: buprenorphine and naloxone. Buprenorphine is considered a partial opioid agonist; this means its effect is less intense than a full opioid—opiate addicts will not experience a high when taking this medication properly—and users will not experience withdrawal symptoms from stopping opiates. Buprenorphine works by binding tightly to the opiate receptors in the brain, which also prevents effects from other opiates; this means that if the user took buprenorphine and a full opioid—such as oxycodone, heroin, morphine, and hydrocodone—the full opioid would not produce the desired effect. Naloxone is an opioid antagonist, or blocker. The naloxone in Suboxone is inactive when the medication is taken as intended, sublingually (under the tongue), but it will cause severe withdrawal symptoms if someone misuses Suboxone by crushing and then injecting or snorting it. In contrast, if you use another opiate on top of methadone, a partial opioid agonist, you can get high and increase the effects of the methadone, dramatically raising the chances of overdose. Methadone is similar to all other opiates but is longer acting, so it is administered once a day in methadone clinics around the country as a replacement opiate for addicts to prevent unmanageable withdrawal symptoms. The drug is prescribed by doctors at the clinics who usually follow strict guidelines to ensure it's safe and consistently used, limiting diversion (giving or selling it to others). Methadone can be prescribed by private physicians, but the restrictions on prescribing it are tighter than those for prescribing Suboxone. For example, when prescribed privately outside of a methadone clinic, methadone can only be used to treat pain, not addiction.

Again, because of its similarities to other full opiates, methadone poses a higher risk of overdose and misuse than Suboxone. Suboxone has a partial or ceiling effect when it attaches to the opiate receptor sites in the brain, decreasing the likelihood of an overdose. Before taking Suboxone, you need to be off of opiates for about forty-eight hours, depending on how long acting the opiate is. For example, it may be started twenty-four hours after heroin and other short-acting opiates have been used and seventy-two hours after using methadone, which is longer acting.

Many clinicians prefer Suboxone to methadone as a replacement therapy for the chronic relapsing addict, and it was originally reported to be "abuse-proof." That turned out not to be completely true: There is some euphoria associated with

Suboxone if you have not been using other opiates. Because of this, Suboxone is sometimes being illicitly diverted—some addicts are selling it for profit, having received legitimate prescriptions for it from their doctors, or are hoarding the drug for when they are in withdrawal from other opiates they are using.

In an August 2013 article, Peter Luongo, executive director of the Institute for Research, Education, and Training in Addictions in Pittsburgh, told Richard Gazarik of Trib Total Media that Suboxone "was never meant to be a stand-alone drug treatment. It's meant to be used with counseling methods."[45] This often includes cognitive behavioral therapy where you learn to change your addictive thinking patterns supplemented by Twelve Step peer support for ongoing recovery.

Unlike methadone, which must be obtained from clinics that monitor its use, Suboxone can be prescribed by a doctor who has taken an eight-hour class about the drug. The doctor is not required to be a specialist in addiction. The government approved this method of dispensing the drug because of the country's increasing opiate-dependence problem and to improve access for the growing number of patients. In his article on the explosion and misuse of Suboxone in Pennsylvania, Gazarik reported that under federal law, the number of patients a doctor would be allowed to treat with Suboxone was capped at thirty for the first year the doctor is licensed to prescribe the drug. But as demand skyrocketed for Suboxone prescriptions, the cap was increased to one hundred patients for the second year.

Some patients have jeopardized their own sobriety by selling their Suboxone on the street, which is why the American Society of Addiction Medicine has put guidelines in place for closer monitoring of people being prescribed Suboxone.

There are some doctors who will only take private pay patients so they don't have to deal with insurance, but most who do this are forced to by insurance companies who still won't adequately reimburse for Suboxone treatment.

Lisa is doing well on maintenance Suboxone. She sees a therapist weekly through the state and is also on two antidepressants. It seems to be working for her. I know her well, and when she relapses, it is not pretty; she is nonfunctional within a week. But she buys her Suboxone on the street because she has no insurance and cannot afford the fee for a private doctor and the requirement to come in monthly and pay that fee again and again. I worry about her buying Suboxone on the street; it seems to be just a step away from the heroin dealer.

I mentioned earlier how I had used the same drug, but the injectable form of Suboxone, Subutex, which has only the opiate component in it, buprenorphine. During my three-month stint in rehab, there was much debate among the doctors as to whether I would be able to be detoxed successfully from it, having been using it for two years. In the end, it took a long, hard six weeks before I was finally free of buprenorphine. I'm not clear on my doctor's motives for prescribing an injectable opiate to me, a known addict, in the first place, although I certainly played a role in becoming addicted to buprenorphine.

Once you have achieved sobriety and are detoxed off of opiates, naltrexone, either taken orally or by injection, will completely block the effects of any opiates taken. If you use an opiate, you will get no effect from it because naltrexone blocks the opiate receptor sites in your brain. This will buy you some time until your craving for opiates subsides. When you take naltrexone you should have some kind of social support and encouragement to help keep you from stopping it so you can use again and get the full effect of an opiate. Again, there are no magic medical bullets.

There is a well-respected outpatient clinic in the Washington-Baltimore area called the Kolmac Clinic owned by Dr. George Kolodner. He told me that nationally there is no dispute among addiction professionals that Suboxone can work wonderfully in an addict's life as an added tool to increase the odds of sobriety. But the patient must be supervised, with random urine tests and therapy to ensure the drug is not being abused.

He added that many people in recovery have a bias against addicts who are on opiate replacement therapy, considering them not "clean." But there is hope: Narcotics Anonymous meetings are popping up just for folks successfully on opiate replacement therapy. Dr. Kolodner also told me that the opiate addicts who are having the hardest time staying sober are the ones with intense trauma in their past, and that Suboxone seems to "soothe" the part of the brain where that trauma exists. Bill Wilson wrote in 1939 that we should utilize all methods in the pursuit of sobriety.[46] I think he would approve of any modern-day solutions. Let's give those doing well on opiate replacement therapy the respect they deserve and celebrate their increasingly functional lives in the face of this tough disease.

Cognitive-Behavioral Therapy

In a large mansion in south Florida, I was ready to meet a beautiful and financially blessed famous mom. Actually, I am never completely ready and am always a little scared, but as always, I march forward. In the end, however, this woman was just another person with a disease that has neither boundaries nor bias in whom it afflicts. But the more insulated a person is by wealth and fame, the more difficult it can be to break through the denial and get help. The bigger the ego, the louder the disease seems to whisper in the ear that it is okay to live with addiction, as their money and fame create a false sense of security unavailable to the average person. In addition, the people who surround celebrities are often reluctant to confront them with the problem for various reasons. Sometimes this has to do with finances—not lack of money, but fear by those who depend on the famous people for financial support that they could be cut off if they challenge them about their addiction. Sometimes it is emotional, and sometimes it is simply that, like many average families, they just do not know what to do. Then they call me.

I entered the foyer, which was the size of my whole house, with her dad, husband, in-laws, and one courageous friend who was willing to risk her friendship with "Missy." (As with other people in this book, I've changed her name and any identifying features in her story to protect her anonymity.) Like many of my interventionist groups, this little army hovered behind me, trying to hide, but I didn't let them stay there for long. I always tell the group members to hug the patient right after I have introduced myself.

"Hi, my name is Joani," I said, as Missy looked at me in a way that seemed to ask, "Do I know you?" I took her hand in both of mine. She was in sweats, with her hair pulled back into a ponytail, looking like a mom just home from the gym. Amazingly, even though I'm a little nervous, my hands are always warm and dry, even when I meet someone famous like this. And the truth is, when I first meet a new patient, I am looking at the disease, not the person. The human being before me is, for the most part, gone, their mind—and some would say their soul—stolen by the disease of addiction. What I enjoy so much about the letters that friends and family write to the addict prior to an intervention is that they give me a wonderful glimpse of the person we are fighting to get back.

"I am here today, Missy, because all of these folks care about you and are worried for you," I said. "Today is all about the love they feel for you." I turned to the group, who looked like they were attending a funeral, even though I had told them over and over that this was a joyous day, and said, "Give Missy a big hug, you guys." And they did, one by one.

So far Missy was quiet. I suspected she had been expecting this intervention. Either that or her mind was quietly and quickly working overtime to figure out how to get out of this developing situation. This is not rocket science: people figure out at electric speed when I enter the room that an intervention is taking place.

After all the hugs, I said, "Let's sit down and I will explain who I am and what is going on." "I am not going to another fucking rehab" were Missy's first words, which exploded out of her pretty mouth like a bomb. "Crap!" I thought, although I stayed calm. With all I knew about the difficulties of dealing with celebrities, why did I think this one would be easy? Maybe it was because the first celebrity I worked with was a man who cried his eyes out during the whole intervention. When we pulled into rehab, he said, "Do you think anybody will recognize me?" I just stared at him as if to say, "You're kidding, right?" And for the first time, he and I laughed—it was one of those really good belly laughs. "Don't worry," I told him. "Everybody who ends up in rehab is a total mess—they will only take notice of you for a few minutes before they are preoccupied with their own shit." Famous people become normalized very quickly. You are given notice that this person will be on campus and if he or she will be in your group. The staff reminds the other patients of the rights of privacy and the laws that back them up, but more than that, you are told to give the celebrity the gift of normalcy so he or she, too, can take full advantage of the treatment program. You realize quickly that such people are very much like the rest of the human race.

When they are out in public, however, celebrities are treated differently, which makes it more difficult for them to attend public recovery groups. That, I believe, is the biggest obstacle celebrities face when trying to recover from this disease: they are not afforded the same opportunity as others to take advantage of meetings. I replied to Missy, "The choice of what you do today is completely yours." I was giving her back the control. This is one of the most important first steps an interventionist can take to keep the situation calm. When a person feels in command of the situation, it is easier to calm down and hear that people really care and that they now have options.

It was a tough intervention. Missy's resistance boiled down to this: "I have tried Twelve Step rehabs and meetings over and over, and they don't work for me. It is a waste of my time to try another." We had arranged for Missy to attend a very well-respected rehab that was Twelve Step based. I now had to switch it to get the job done. "Where is your computer, Missy? Can I show you a rehab I have used many times, and they use cognitive therapy instead of the Twelve Steps?" "Sure," she said. I pulled it up on the computer. It was beautiful, *and* it had a music studio, which appealed to her greatly.

It is a small rehab with a limited number of beds, but as luck would have it, one was available, and Missy agreed to go because they used a cognitive approach rather than the Twelve Steps. We hopped into her private plane, and off we went. I used to be a Twelve Step purist, thinking it was the only way to get and stay clean. But because some people just do not agree with the methodology of the Twelve Steps, which are spiritual in nature, I needed to look beyond my own personal bias for legitimate alternatives. And I have seen a number of folks achieve successful sobriety with cognitive behavioral therapy, or CBT. This approach still involves developing a solid relapse prevention plan and ongoing peer or therapeutic support, especially in the first year after treatment.

A comprehensive program using CBT involves not only training patients in replacing their addictive thinking with positive, reality-based thoughts but often utilizes mindfulness meditation techniques for stress management and educational programming to teach social skills, many times taught through role-playing behavior with clinician and group feedback. CBT is designed to help patients recognize and avoid the thought processes, situations, and behaviors associated with substance abuse. It teaches them refusal skills—how to turn down drugs when they're offered—and how to develop better problem-solving and coping skills.

Studies have shown that CBT is effective for both adolescents and adults, and for people with co-occurring psychiatric diagnoses. It is most effective if followed up with mutual support groups, which can be Twelve Step based if the person feels motivated to go in that direction. Secular support groups are also available. Some CBT patients gravitate to SMART Recovery and its support groups. At its website (www.smartrecovery.org), SMART Recovery says that its approach

- Teaches self-empowerment and self-reliance.
- Provides meetings that are educational, supportive, and include open discussions.
- Encourages individuals to recover from addiction and alcohol abuse and live satisfying lives.
- Teaches techniques for self-directed change.
- Supports the scientifically informed use of psychological treatments and legally prescribed psychiatric and addiction medication.

- Works on substance abuse, alcohol abuse, addiction, and drug abuse as complex maladaptive behaviors with possible physiological factors.
- Evolves as scientific knowledge in addiction recovery evolves.
- Differs from Alcoholics Anonymous, Narcotics Anonymous, and other Twelve Step programs.

Another group not based on the Twelve Steps is Rational Recovery, but these groups are not as widely available and research comparing their effectiveness to the more established Twelve Step support groups like AA and NA is inconclusive.

Two months after Missy entered rehab, I was at the facility dropping off another patient and the staff told me that she was in one of the common rooms. I peeked my head around the corner. Missy saw me, jumped up, and came to the door. She was in much better physical shape than when I first met her— her hug almost hurt. She went on to tell me how comfortable she was at this rehab and that their treatment approach was a wonderful fit for her. Two years later, Missy is still sober, and every time I come across her name in print or see her on TV, she makes me smile.

• • •

Next we will look at new laws aimed at counteracting the rise in prescription opiate addiction.

10

LAWS THAT MIGHT HELP STEM THE TIDE OF PRESCRIPTION DRUG DEATHS

This growing opiate abuse epidemic boggles the mind. There's this: The total number of prescriptions for opioid pain relievers in the United States almost tripled in a twenty-year period, soaring from 76 million in 1991 to 210 million in 2010.[47] And I've already mentioned this startling recent development: An American is now more likely to die of an overdose of medication prescribed by a doctor or obtained on the street than to die on the highway.

Just as we have passed legislation to make our roadways safer—with DWI and underage drinking laws plus laws requiring seat belt usage and air bags in new vehicles—legislation is now on the books and further action is being considered to stem the tide of deaths from prescription drugs. To date, this includes laws that restrict prescriptions of controlled drugs, their use, and the practice of doctor shopping and buying medications and drugs over the Internet.

Heroin has long been illegal, and the "war on drugs" has

tried repeatedly to stem the tide with legal consequences for both use and distribution of this drug. But as we learned earlier, just as prescription opiates are getting more expensive and harder to obtain, heroin has become widely available, inexpensive, and use is surging in this country. Somewhere deep in other countries, the people who fuel heroin importation to the United States have a keen eye on a growing market for their product. It is big business, and for the most part, these folks in the shadows are not stupid. I imagine they are aware of the financial benefits they receive because of our tightening up on prescription drug availability.

It would be impractical here to cover all the state laws and pending legislation aimed at curbing prescription drug abuse. You can find a comprehensive list of them at the CDC's Prescription Drug Overdose web page, www.cdc.gov /HomeandRecreationalSafety/Poisoning/laws/index.html. I do, however, want to highlight and, more importantly, talk about the laws that I think will help.

In my experience, doctor shopping was like gambling. As I cruised urgent care centers, telephone directories, and innocent neighbors who were doctors, the chase was as exciting as swallowing, snorting, or shooting the opiate. But many states are enacting legislation to stop this deadly game. Some states are creating databases on all controlled drugs purchased at pharmacies that link your driver's license number to all such prescriptions you pick up at the store. The pharmacies are then required to report your driver's license number to a government agency. The database can then tag you if you frequent multiple pharmacies. I think the use of phony IDs might be a way to get around this law, but it is not foolproof and would only slow the process down a little for anyone who tried it.

Some people argue that laws like this one are an overreach

of government authority and a breach of our constitutional rights to privacy and confidentiality. But given the rising body count associated with opioid abuse, I personally do not oppose such laws. And if you have nothing to hide, I don't think you have anything to fear.

Florida, dubbed the unofficial capital of pill mills, has passed laws that give the state oversight over privately owned clinics, facilities, or offices that employ one or more physicians who primarily treat chronic pain patients with controlled medications and that advertise in any medium—such as print, TV, or the Internet—for pain management. Such facilities must register with the Florida Department of Health. The key word here is "advertise." Word of mouth among addicts is extensive, and many times it is all the advertising you need to promote your services. Another addict once asked me, "Joani, why are you still taking Lorcet? The Tylenol will fuck your liver up. Switch to OxyContin—pure oxycodone, a better high, and no Tylenol. There is this doctor who will prescribe anything for you easily." She gave me his name; I made an appointment the next day.

Virginia has a law that allows prescription monitoring data to be shared with drug monitoring programs in other states. Professionally, I find Virginia to be one of the toughest states in the mid-Atlantic region when it comes to prosecuting those who break laws related to alcohol and other drug use. Politicians in the state run their campaigns around promising and enforcing tougher laws on substance abuse. Many crimes related to substance abuse in Virginia carry mandatory sentences, and judges have no leeway in deciding the penalties for the offenses committed. In my work, this means I cannot go to court and tell a judge that a patient has been compliant with an intervention and has done his or her time in rehab in hopes of reducing the legal consequences for that person, such as time in prison.

Often, the best that an attorney can do is to arrange to have a court appearance pushed back after a client makes bail, in order to give the patient time to go to rehab. Many times the judge will praise such efforts by the addict and offer words of encouragement: "Good for you! The court is pleased that you have taken proactive action in treating your disease." But, the judge will add, "according to our state law, the mandatory sentence for your offense is . . ."

Many of the opiate addicts I have done interventions on who are facing jail time are relatively young, usually in their twenties. Once these young people are released from prison, their parents who are financially able to will, on my advice, immediately transfer their kids back to the rehab they were in before their incarceration. This helps reinforce what the patient initially learned in treatment and reduces the risk of the disease flaring up. But I must emphasize, few families have the financial means to do this.

A young twenty-something named Daniel who lived in Virginia was in this position. His lawyer arranged to have his court date pushed back, and he spent three months in treatment before facing a judge. When I dropped him off at rehab, his last words to me were, "Get the fuck away from me." After rehab, Daniel returned home for a short time, served one year in prison for heroin possession, and then immediately returned to the rehab center. One day my cell phone rang.

"Hello, Joani. This is Daniel. Remember me?"

How could I forget him and the sweet parting serenade he spit at me? "Hey, buddy, of course I do! How are you?" He took a deep breath, "Good, good. I did my time in Virginia and I am back in the rehab." He hesitated. I waited, sensing there was something else he wanted to tell me; also, I get a lot of these calls. "I am sitting with my therapist using his phone, and I wanted to say I am sorry for treating you so disrespectfully. It was wrong of me. Really, I am sorry."

"Daniel," I said, "your call and apology mean the world to me. Thank you so much—you have made my day!" And I meant it. DJ, a therapist at the La Hacienda treatment facility in Texas, always emphasized that saying you are sorry is not enough when making amends to someone. What you need to say and feel, and what the other person wants to hear, is that your behavior and actions were wrong.

It's a few years later now, and I hear Daniel is doing well. His parents set tough boundaries the day of the intervention— it was face me or the homeless shelter—and Daniel took it all the way to the mat before relenting and agreeing to rehab. And it has ended well.

In the mid-Atlantic, for better or worse, there are numerous small states that are very close to each other. And many savvy addicts regularly travel across state lines to jurisdictions where laws are not as restrictive on buying, using, and distributing controlled opiates. Virginia, Maryland, and the District of Columbia border each other, and I see many people who take advantage of Maryland's and the district's more liberal laws to get their drugs.

Farther up the East Coast, Rhode Island has a law that prohibits physicians, dentists, osteopaths, chiropractors, and even veterinarians from prescribing controlled narcotics unless a physical exam has been done on the person or animal first. I think this might reduce the number of fake weekend calls to dentists and doctors—and personally speaking, my five-pound dog, Lucy, was not worth the effort to call my veterinarian. Her small size would only result in an *extremely* low dose of narcotics being prescribed to her. But there is not an addict around who cannot fake his or her way through a physical exam in order to get narcotics. And if the doctor is profit motivated, you barely have to put any effort into it.

Tamper-resistant prescription pads are the law in Tennessee, once the epicenter of the surge in OxyContin abuse and addiction. It is now against state law for a pharmacist to fill any prescription that is not on tamper-resistant paper. The federal government requires all Medicaid and Medicare controlled-narcotic prescriptions to be written on these security pads as well. Under a federal law that went into effect in 2008 that states implement and enforce, the pads on which all such Medicaid and Medicare prescriptions are written must contain at least one tamper-resistant feature. The main feature of these pads is that if they are photocopied, the word "void" or "illegal" appears on them. If someone tries to alter the prescription by writing on it with different ink than what was used originally, the chemical nature of the tamper-resistant paper causes a change in color, making it obvious the prescription has been tampered with.

To see how hard it is to obtain such a pad, I recently went online and tried to order one from a company that makes them. I had to have a Drug Enforcement Administration (DEA) number for my first order; thereafter, the company said, my name and DEA number would be on file and I would not need to repeat the application process. DEA numbers are not hard to obtain from a doctor's or dentist's office. Unfortunately, some doctors leave their prescription pads in a drawer in the patient exam room for their convenience. In my using days, I lifted more of them than I would like to admit.

All of these laws will slow things down, but addicts are persistent in their pursuit of prescription drugs, and there is often a way around such laws if you try hard enough. I feel ambivalent writing about how to do that, but I hope my comments present a cautionary tale for prescribers and pharmacies, and bring awareness that we need to look at the problem from different angles and put our resources elsewhere.

And there is hope.

A California law passed in October 2013 and in effect in certain counties until January 1, 2016, can help save lives in the battle against drug overdose deaths. Assembly Bill 635 basically allows any health care worker who can prescribe opiates to also prescribe naloxone to a patient or to the patient's loved ones and family.[48] Moreover, the professional prescribing and the person administering naloxone cannot be held liable for either dispensing or administering the drug. Naloxone, also known as Narcan, is an opiate antagonist that reverses the effects of a full opiate, like heroin or OxyContin, in cases of overdose and imminent death. Naloxone, which we talked about in chapter 9 as an ingredient in Suboxone, blocks the effect of the opiate by binding to the same receptor in the brain as the opiate and knocking it off. It reverses the overdose, and if the victim has stopped breathing, allows him or her to begin breathing again. When naloxone is given as an injection or nasal spray, the overdose may be reversed immediately; with the nasal spray, the victim can wake up in as little as two to five minutes.

Here is part of the bill as it was originally written:

> *This bill would . . . authorize a licensed health care provider who is permitted by law to prescribe an opioid antagonist [naloxone] and is acting with reasonable care to prescribe and subsequently dispense or distribute an opioid antagonist for the treatment of an opioid overdose to a person at risk of an opioid-related overdose or a family member, friend, or other person in a position to assist a person at risk of an opioid-related overdose.*

I can almost hear some people yelling at me right now, calling this "The Enabler Bill." But it is not about enabling—it is about saving the life of someone who is going to use opiates no matter the circumstances. Some people will ask why a health care professional would prescribe opiates to someone suspected of abusing the medication. Well, sometimes doctors cannot tell if they are prescribing for true pain or addiction. Also, some extreme chronic pain patients are legitimately on high doses of opiates that are potentially dangerous.

If this bill had been in effect in the state where I practiced nursing, it could have potentially helped me to save a life.

• • •

When I was working at a state rehab as an RN, a patient who had been on an outing returned to the center. I believe that over time, she had obtained prescription opiates while she was out on passes. Back at the rehab, she consumed the opiate pills, misjudging her tolerance level for the drug, something that decreases quickly after one is detoxed.

I was in the kitchen eating an oatmeal cookie and was in my seventh month of pregnancy with my son, Max, when I heard the other female patients hysterically yelling for my help. I screamed to the cook who was in the kitchen with me to get more staff up to the second floor. I bounded up the stairs, ripping the CPR mask off the wall as I rounded a corner, instinctively knowing it would be needed.

Melanie was on the bed, unconscious. I felt her neck—no pulse. Putting my hand on her chest, I felt no movement to indicate she was breathing. Her skin was still pink and felt warm to the touch. She could not have been out for long. "Tawana, get her feet. I need her on the floor," I instructed another patient. I needed Melanie on a hard surface to start CPR. Jose, a counselor, came running into the room. Looking up, I simply

said, "I will do compressions; you do respirations," as I handed him the CPR respiratory mask. (I was pregnant and did not want her saliva in my mouth, even though the CPR mask has a one-way valve to prevent that.)

"Call 911," I yelled to security. Getting a weak pulse after doing chest compressions for a few minutes, I began to feel hopeful. Her chest rhythmically rose and fell as Jose breathed his own oxygen into her lungs. The paramedics arrived, but a good fifteen minutes had gone by. "Move," one paramedic barked at me. This was no time for small talk, but I felt a little insulted. I was forty-four years old and seven months pregnant, and doing chest compressions for fifteen minutes was not easy. But I was also relieved.

"Tell me what we have," he said, as he ripped her shirt open and tore her bra in half. I remember feeling embarrassed for her as she lay exposed before all of us. Feeling her pulse and getting nothing, he pulled out the cardiac paddles and shocked her chest in hopes of bringing her back.

"She just got back from a patient outing," I said. "She is an opiate addict."

"Narcan," he yelled to his partner. Narcan, also known as naloxone, is an opioid antagonist that could reverse an opiate overdose, was premixed in a syringe. The paramedic removed the cap of the syringe with his mouth and jammed the needle deep into Melanie's thigh. I watched the heart monitor closely, holding my own breath, hoping to see her come back, but it did not happen. Melanie died at age thirty-four.

The paramedic looked at me and said, "Another dead junkie." He did not say it in a derogatory tone, but I hate that word. What do you call a diabetic in ketoacidosis, a condition that can occur when the blood sugar is out of control? I threw the CPR mask into his lap.

"Listen, she is not a junkie. She is a human being who just

died from addiction, which is a chronic, progressive, and fatal disease," I spat out as I stormed out of the room. As a walked down the hall, I heard one of the staff say to the paramedic, "She is pregnant," to try to explain my outburst. But it was not the pregnancy and my perceived hormonal condition that caused me to yell at the paramedic. It was my passion for this misunderstood disease and the lack of respect I feel when addicts are still called names.

In my mind, I kept seeing Melanie's nine-year-old daughter who visited her the weekend before. Melanie had patiently braided her daughter's hair—it was like a freeze-frame in my mind as I returned to the nurse's station to quickly write down my documentation of the event before Melanie's body was taken to the hospital.

As I was catching my own breath and calming my nerves, the nursing assistant placed on my desk all the bottles of opiates he had found in Melanie's purse. He knew I would need the prescription information for my nurse's notes. And to my still-amazed addict mind, I looked inside the bottles to see if there were any opiates left for me to divert. I was pregnant and had been sober a good while. I had just pounded on a dead girl's chest, seeing as up close as possible the consequences of abusing opiates, witnessing the ultimate price—death—and that addict son of a bitch who resides in my brain was still searching for my own demise, trying to lure me in with its sick lies. I took the bottles and threw them at the wall, screaming to an invisible but real enemy, "Leave me the fuck alone"—knowing that it might never completely let me be.

Then I went into the nurse's bathroom, put the toilet seat down, sat, and wept—for Melanie, for me, and for all the misunderstood addicts who are dogged by this disease that defies all logic. Dr. Bob, cofounder of Alcoholics Anonymous, wrote that his cravings never left him completely. The other co-founder, Bill W., also wrote that good recovery is when you are in a place of neutrality, and I am there about 90 percent of the time. It is that other 10 percent that poses a real threat to my life.

The events at the state rehab happened years ago, before such facilities regularly kept Narcan on hand. I have often wondered if I could have saved Melanie if I had had that life-saving medication. I am finding that life is full of unanswerable questions. California's bill 635, and other such legislation around the country, would have had my vote because Narcan must be available to all clinics and individuals when there is a possibility of opiate overdose.

• • •

Other legislation aimed at preventing deaths from prescription drugs targets what used to be one of my favorite ways to obtain prescription narcotics while traveling out of my home state. These bills—under different numbers and names according to the state, and either passed or pending—make it illegal for a health care worker to fill lost, stolen, or destroyed prescriptions of controlled narcotics for a person traveling from another state.

Thus, when a well-dressed and educated mom like me shows up at an out-of-state urgent care center with a baby on her hip and a huge scar on her back and offers a fairy tale of how "I left my pain medication at home," a health care worker is not legally allowed to give me a replacement prescription for controlled opiates. What's tragic here is that there are real chronic pain patients, not addicts who are abusing the system, to whom this might happen. And they suffer because of those of us who misuse the health care system.

One solution for a real pain patient would be to call your

personal doctor and ask him or her to call in a narcotic prescription at a pharmacy chain. Then you can fill it at the same chain out of state. No doubt this practice is abused now, and legislation in the future might be aimed at halting it.

I do not believe that the ever-increasing number of laws intended to curb prescription drug abuse will end the ultimate problem of addiction to opiates. We're already seeing how many prescription drug addicts will acquire opiates by switching to street heroin that is increasingly available and is cheaper. And it is more dangerous: you never really know what you are getting when drugs are bought on the street.

The supply will never go away. Hunting down and prosecuting the profit-motivated doctors and pharmacies, the street criminals, and the drug consumers reminds me of playing Whac-A-Mole: you smack one problem down, and two more pop up. Billions have been spent on the war on drugs, both legal and illegal, and yet current statistics reflect a sobering reality: the problem of opiate dependence has increased over time, not decreased.

As Alex Garcia-Barbon, detox program director of Southwest Florida Addiction Services, explained in a 2012 article published in the *Fort Myers Florida Weekly*: "Two to three years ago, the majority of our patients would have been alcohol patients, 45 and over. Today about 75 percent of our patients are opiate patients. And the age group has decreased. Now, the majority of patients are between 19 and 34."[49]

Real pain patients are victims who are often left in limbo by being undertreated for their suffering, feeling the consequences of a corrupt system of narcotic use and distribution. "Someone who has never abused alcohol or other drugs would be extremely unlikely to become addicted to opioid pain medicines, particularly if he or she is older," in the words of Russell K.

Portenoy, chair of the Department of Pain Medicine and Palliative Care at Beth Israel Medical Center in New York.[50]

So what do we do? I believe that because the war on drugs has failed the way we are currently waging it, we need to put more of our resources at the front end of addiction. We need to spend more on educating young people about this disease and preventing it. Yes, we have done some of this, but we need to step it up. Start educating earlier—at elementary school age—and repeat the education often. Imbed the information into the minds and consciousness of our youth.

We also need better health care coverage for addiction. We should use more tax revenue from cigarettes, alcohol—and even medical marijuana as more states legalize it—for medical treatment for this disease. We also need to get our young people into treatment sooner; the longer a person is addicted, the more the brain is affected and the more complicated the disease becomes. Funding for public assistance needs to be increased to provide lower income families the same opportunities for treatment as those at the other end of the economic spectrum. The haves and have-nots need to be afforded the same level of care for this disease, and I am not just talking about the extremely poor but the middle class as well. We've already seen how many middle-class families cannot afford the price tag for quality treatment. These are areas in which I think new laws could be effective in the battle against drug overdose deaths.

In October 2013 word came of another attempt to curb the abuse of opiates. The Center for Drug Evaluation and Research, part of the U.S. Food and Drug Administration (FDA), announced that by early December, the FDA planned to recommend that the U.S. Department of Health and Human Services reclassify hydrocodone combination products into the more

University, *Addiction Medicine: Closing the Gap between Science and Practice*, found that, "Once an individual develops addiction, changes in the brain's reward circuitry may remain even after cessation of substance use. These changes leave addicted individuals vulnerable to physiological and environmental cues that they have associated with substance use, increasing the risk of relapse. In these cases, addiction is a chronic disease—like heart disease, hypertension, diabetes and asthma."[53]

The study goes on to say that young people who start drug use early are at extreme risk of developing lifelong struggles with addiction due to the injury or insult to the young brain that is not completely developed. "Although the reasons are not yet clear," it says, "some individuals may experience one episode in which their symptoms meet clinical diagnostic criteria for addiction and be nonsymptomatic thereafter. In many cases, however, addiction manifests as a chronic disease—a persistent or long-lasting illness—which requires ongoing professional treatment and management. This may be due to a preexisting brain dysfunction or to changes that occur in the brain in response to repeated exposure to addictive substances which increase the vulnerability of the individual to relapse, even after cessation of substance use."

And a statement that accompanied the study notes that, "In homes, doctors' offices, hospitals, schools, prisons, jails and communities across America, misperceptions about addiction are undermining medical care. Although advances in neuroscience, brain imaging and behavioral research clearly show that addiction is a complex brain disease, today the disease of addiction is still often misunderstood as a moral failing, a lack of willpower, a subject of shame and disgust."

In June 2010, researchers reported on a follow-up study they conducted on 109 opiate addicts who had been in an inpatient setting for detoxification and treatment.[54] The researchers looked at the rate of relapse after discharge and sought to find the factors linked with daily return to opiate use. Ninety-nine of the 109 patients, or 91 percent, reported relapse after treatment, and 64 of those people, or 59 percent, relapsed within one week of discharge. The researchers looked at variables in early relapse and found significant common denominators in age—the younger the patient, the higher the rate of early relapse—as well as greater heroin use prior to treatment, a history of using needles to inject opiates, and failure to follow up with aftercare. The patients who completed the entire six-week inpatient program lasted much longer before relapsing.

Celebrating Periods of Remission

Like any other chronic condition, addiction rarely abates after a single course of medication or other treatment, or after a single attempt to alter one's lifestyle or behavior. As is true for people with other chronic conditions, people with addiction can have symptom-free periods and periods when the disease recurs. For many patients, this happens multiple times, and still others never achieve effective disease management. In fact, addiction frequently is characterized as a disease where recurrence is virtually inevitable.

That brings me to the so-called chip system, a reward practice used in many recovery programs, such as Alcoholics Anonymous and Narcotics Anonymous. I believe wholeheartedly in giving chips to reward and mark sobriety time in recovery, with one significant exception. Chips, also known as medallions, go back as early as 1942, just a few years after the beginnings of AA. The practice is thought to have started with Doherty S., who originally brought AA to Indianapolis. The custom may have started even earlier with Sister Ignatia, the

nun who helped Dr. Bob Smith get the hospitalization program started at St. Thomas Hospital in Akron, Ohio, that
treated alcoholics. When alcoholics were preparing to leave
St. Thomas, she gave them a Sacred Heart medallion to represent the commitment they were making to God, AA, and
recovery. She also told them that if they were going to drink,
she expected them to first return the medallion to her.[55] I get
goosebumps when I read about this nun. Alcoholics have a
long history of being misunderstood and judged, and here was
a nun, not an alcoholic herself, showing compassion to those
afflicted with this disease during a time when alcoholics were
so maligned. Going back even earlier, the custom can be traced
to the Catholic temperance movement of 1830s Ireland. Tokens
of healing and the use of medals were common in Roman
Catholicism. During the temperance movement, tokens were
given as part of a renunciation ritual. The AA use of chips may
derive from these customs, stripped of their overtly Roman
Catholic content.

The chip system is alive in today's rooms of recovery. A person presented with a token is met with enthusiastic hugs and
applause. It is a special moment, and it plays a big part in en-
couraging recovering people to continue their quest for sobriety. The first token awarded is the twenty-four-hour chip,
received when entering recovery. Then come the one-month
chip, the two-month chip, and so on, until the person reaches
one year of sobriety. (One year is momentous for another reason: you usually get a cake to go with your chip!) Then eigh-
teen months, two years, and thereafter annually.

This is what I don't agree with: if a person's addiction recurs
after, say, twelve years of sobriety, that person is expected to go
into the rooms of recovery, pick up a twenty-four-hour chip,
and start counting all over again—wiping away all those years

of successful recovery! Look at it this way: if a person is cancer free for twelve years and then the cancer comes back, that does not mean that those twelve cancer-free years were not significant! I propose that if the disease rears its ugly head and a person is afflicted once more, when he or she returns to the rooms of recovery, a chip is awarded for "courage and survival" and the person can continue counting where he or she left off. I think this is a much more positive approach and would encourage more folks whose disease recurs to come back to recovery.

I have gone to the funerals of three people whose disease returned and who died as a result. I have often thought that they might have returned to the rooms of recovery if they were given a positive chip—not a twenty-four-hour chip, wiping out their years of successful sobriety. I think positive reinforcement would be much more effective in our efforts to increase our sobriety rates. The founders of AA, Bill Wilson and Dr. Bob Smith, used the words "cunning, baffling, and powerful" to describe the disease of addiction.[56] Even as science can more accurately explain the brain physiology behind it, addiction can still feel cunning for those of us in the grip of its talons, and it can be elusive as we attempt to get our disease back into remission.

Euphoric Recall and Planning for Relapse

It is an ordinary autumn day, complete with colorful leaves, pumpkins adorning porches, and, in the air, the smell of fireplaces heralding the beginning of the season. Once again, this is euphoric recall and it triggers strong opiate cravings for me. The rush of dopamine in the reward system can be medically explained, but I nonetheless feel a deep, indescribable need to use.

I've already described how dopamine is released in the

brain during pleasurable activities, many of which have to do with survival, like eating and sex (nourishment and procreation ensure existence of the species); and I've explained how mood-altering drugs release huge amounts of dopamine and that this is what produces the "high" that people feel. Just like Pavlov's dogs, who had a conditioned response to the ringing of a bell that signaled food would follow, people afflicted with an addict brain have a conditioned response to the drugs that produce dopamine. Euphoric recall will happen when an activity, time of year, stress, the presence of drugs or paraphernalia, smell, or anything else associated with drug use is reproduced; and just like salivating dogs waiting for food after a bell is rung, the addict is reminded of the drug that produced pleasure and a craving sets in.

Now you are screwed. Or not. The question is, how does the individual get through this invisible but powerful event, which literally has the potential to kill the addict? As the *Big Book* of Alcoholics Anonymous so accurately told us seventy-five years ago, "The main problem of the alcoholic centers in his mind, rather than in his body."[57] This means that while detoxification and physical addiction can be long over, the addict still might pick up the drug again.

Much of the research on recovery confirms that those who are eventually successful at establishing long-term recovery after treatment and relapses have a relapse prevention plan. Earlier, in chapter 6, I introduced what a typical plan includes, but it bears repeating:

- going to peer support meetings regularly
- having a sponsor, therapist, or mentor who can be a guide in your recovery program
- staying away from the people, places, and things associated with using

- avoiding stress and negative feelings whenever possible; when they occur, dealing with them using techniques like meditation and positive self-talk
- getting professional help, including nonaddictive medications for co-occurring psychiatric conditions like depression, anxiety, and trauma
- not isolating and getting involved in service work
- developing a spiritual life that includes reliance on a Higher Power, such as a Twelve Step program and group, nature, family and community, or the God of your understanding if you're religious

Appendix A presents a guide for dealing with the challenges of the first five days after treatment, which will also be useful for the early days after a relapse.

• • •

The girl has had one year of solid recovery. She has a service job of answering phones at the local AA intergroup office and attends meetings almost daily. She has worked the Twelve Steps with a sponsor and in a Sunday group setting. But the smell of the fireplaces is stalking her. As daytime turns to dusk, her need for narcotics feels irresistible. Again, from the Big Book: "We are unable, at certain times, to bring into our consciousness with sufficient force the memory of the suffering and humiliation of even a week or a month ago."[58]

She tells herself she is just going to take a leisurely walk around the neighborhood. Soon, as if by an invisible transport, she shows up on the porch of her friend the doctor to ask for a prescription for back pain. He looks at her with so much concern and is silent until he yells over his shoulder to his family, "I will be right back."

Taking her hand, he walks back toward her house, but they take an unexpected left turn. There is the "Red House," the area AA intergroup office. He walks her inside, and by now the girl has tears streaming down her face from embarrassment and frustration. They sit in chairs; the man answering the phones looks their way and instinctively seems to know to stay at bay.

The doctor takes both of the girl's hands in his.

"Joani," he says, "you are safe here. This moment of desire will pass," and he reaches for a tissue.

"But it will return," she replies angrily.

"Yes, it might, but it will lessen in time. Think how it ends up, where you will be if you start taking narcotics again." In the rooms of recovery, this is known as "think the drink through."

Moments pass, and the girl does start to feel safe. The rooms of recovery are like garlic hanging around your neck to keep the blood-sucking vampires away.

The doctor remembers a conversation we had about Father Martin, a recovering Catholic priest and one of the founders of the rehab Father Martin's Ashley. "Tell me again about Father Martin," he says gently.

A year before while at the rehab, I chased Father Martin around the campus on a Sunday when he had just stopped by to say hello to everyone. He was that kind of person: on his day off, he would show up at the rehab—in his sweats that he made a point of telling me were from Bloomingdale's—just to hang out with us. I wanted to convince him that "rehab" did not necessarily help, citing an example of someone who died at rehab.

"Joani baloney, not everyone is going to survive this deal," he casually said to me. Then, with a gleam in his eye, he turned around on his way to his car and added, "But you are."

"He said I was going to survive this disease," I say to the doctor as I wipe tears from my cheeks.

For that day I was safe. The doctor, the room of recovery, and the memory of Father Martin were my salvation on this day of craving.

• • •

It will not be my last temptation as my mind twists and turns with this chronic illness. But with years of sobriety, I have learned other tricks or methods to moderate this invisible but powerful phenomenon that threatens my life. I will share those simple but effective tools in the last chapter, but first I want to write about another phenomenon, one that has to do with a grocery cart.

DRY DRUNK AND A GROCERY CART

First, my soapbox: I hate the word "drunk" almost as much as I hate the word "junkie." Alcoholics often use the term "drunk" like other addicts use the term "junkie" in a self-deprecating way to keep themselves humble, but to people outside recovery these terms still carry negative connotations. Again, there are no other terms that have derogatory associations to describe other diseases. For example, we don't use unflattering words to label a multiple sclerosis patient who suffers a flare-up.

Having said that, the term "dry drunk" is so widely recognized that I had to use it to title this chapter to be understood. So there it is, "dry drunk."

What Is a Dry Drunk?

As I noted at the beginning of the book, my frequent references to AA instead of Narcotics Anonymous (NA), Pills Anonymous (PA), or Cocaine Anonymous (CA) come from my experience. When you read the basic texts of NA and CA, you see that they use the same Twelve Steps of *Alcoholics Anonymous,* but the substance of alcohol is switched to their members' drug of choice and any of these groups will accept people addicted to any addictive drug. When I returned home from my three months in rehab in Texas, my first recovery meeting was NA. I was so afraid coming home—my son's new diagnosis of autism and my own new sobriety combined to make me feel a sense of futility so strong that I hoped for death. Rehab is a wonderful gift, but you are cloistered and protected in such an environment. Coming home from rehab is a high-risk time that requires attention and the reinforcement of continued treatment as we strive to maintain longer periods of sobriety.

At that first NA meeting after coming home from rehab, I put my head down on the table and just cried. Surely some folks thought I was a spoiled brat, having just had the benefit of three months in a high-end rehab. Or maybe that is my own projection of myself. In any case, I received so much love and support from that roomful of bikers and tattooed kids. They were nothing less than wonderful to me. So why did I not continue with Narcotic Anonymous? To be honest, I ended up gravitating to AA because of the demographics of the people who attend AA meetings near me: they look like me, live in my neighborhood, and I can relate better to them and their lives than to most of the people in NA. There aren't as many meetings available for the other Twelve Step groups so it was inconvenient for me to go to them. Near my home there were AA meetings almost hourly. In open AA meetings, you can talk about any substance as long as alcohol is one of them, and my new group of friends listened to me and my history with prescription drugs with absolutely no objection. When they spoke of vodka and other alcoholic drinks, I just transposed the substance to narcotics in my mind.

I actually found a sponsor in the room of AA who was also a narcotic addict. A sponsor is a person who has at least a couple of years of stable sobriety, is knowledgeable about and has worked the Steps, and is able to support newcomers to help them navigate their new path of recovery. This is a very important part of working a Twelve Step program. So please know that what I say about recovering alcohol addiction applies to opiate addiction as well.

There are a few different definitions of "dry drunk," and it is a controversial subject. The term seems to have originated with (or at least was popularized by) Alcoholics Anonymous, but it is used in a variety of ways. In AA usage, it may refer to an alcoholic (or addict) who is not drinking or using but is not working the Steps. In other usages, the term refers to those in the beginning stages of recovery who have been detoxified and are not drinking or using but still have all the manners, relationships, and associations predictable from their former lives as active addicts. It's someone who is a "baby" in recovery. Other times "dry drunk" is used to describe anyone who used to be a problematic drinker and now abstains but is still unhappy. And yet other times it refers to a person who has all the characteristics of an "alcoholic" but who is able to abstain, even without a recovery program. Some people disagree that there's such a thing as a dry drunk and claim that AA invented the term as a derogatory expression for anyone trying to recover outside of the Twelve Step framework.

Personally, I have never felt it was a term that we folks in recovery use in a derogatory fashion because someone has managed to get sober outside of AA or NA. Speaking for myself, I am happy when anyone manages to get sober and happy, with or without a formal recovery program.

In the article "Is There a 'Dry Drunk' in Your Life?" in the May 14, 2011, issue of *Psychology Today*, Carole Bennett lists six characteristics of a dry drunk that can strike "in the honest light of sobriety" to make life difficult for addicts and for those close to them.[59] These characteristics apply to opiate drug users as well:

1. Resentment at spouses, parents, or whoever has made them stop drinking (or using), or else.

2. Annoyance and frustration with the realization that they can't drink like a "normie" (a normal social drinker)—or ever again.

3. Realization that because of their drinking (or using), they may have not reached their goals, dreams, or potentials, and wondering if it's too late, or if they are even capable of achieving those goals or dreams.

4. Having to accept and take responsibility for the wasted years due to drinking (or using) without an excuse or justification.

5. Anxiety about venturing out or challenging themselves for fear of failure. Alcoholics (or other drug addicts) may not have had any normal life experience with failure and success, which would have made them stronger and wiser. Instead those years were void of dealing with life on life's terms due to the alcohol (or other drug) addiction.

6. Jealousy of others for their stick-to-itiveness, perseverance, and strength. Resenting family members or friends for successfully realizing their dreams and punishing them by not being supportive, questioning their ability, and striving to clip their wings of creativity.

While those six points do describe some of the behaviors that a person abstaining from drugs can exhibit, I prefer the next description, which sums up a quote from Bill Wilson in

Alcoholic Anonymous that I hear in the rooms of recovery over and over: "Our liquor was but a symptom."[60]

In a 2013 article about alcoholism and personality, Dr. Sandra Cabot wrote that alcoholism and opiate addiction are identical in personality characteristics and prevalence of mood disorders.[61] Where they differ is in recurrence of the disease, with opiate addiction having a higher rate than alcoholism. Cabot wrote:

> *Researching alcoholism, personality and mood disorders has helped me in my work with alcohol dependency recovery. Alcoholism is only a symptom of an underlying problem. Put down the drink and you still have the problem—the alcoholic mind and their turbulent emotions. Brain chemistry is genetically linked to alcoholism along with many other mental health issues. Alcoholics are often controlling, manipulative, insecure and depressive. They fear abandonment, they have low self-esteem and are arrested in their emotional development. They have difficulty forming healthy relationships because they never deal with their emotions in a normal adult manner. The terrible emotional pain and suppression they inflict on themselves and those around them, often results in a virtual loss of identity.*

In the rooms of recovery, it's also common to hear another statement, which is a reflection of this apparent lack of self-esteem mixed with narcissism: "I think so little of myself, but I am the only thing I think about."

That brings me to the grocery cart.

DJ is a wonderful teacher and therapist at La Hacienda treatment center in Texas. While addressing a disheveled crew of patients in varying degrees of detox and recovery, he revealed this important insight into our long-term goals as people in recovery: "You are striving to be one of those people who naturally returns their grocery cart back to the store sidewalk." We were all stumped. We momentarily stopped drinking from our coffee cups, holding our drinks in midair as we looked quizzically at each other. "What?" we seemed to ask. "You are supposed to return your grocery cart, not leave it in the parking lot to block another car or to roll down the hill and hit an old lady maybe, denying the underpaid grocery store worker the privilege of taking it back for us?"

Yep, a bunch of self-absorbed, selfish, emotionally immature adults. You can only imagine what it is like to navigate the cafeteria line in treatment facilities with this population of people. Fights break out at the salad bar because someone is "taking too long." The petty drama of rehab can be brutal!

As Bill Wilson wrote in the AA Big Book: "Selfishness—self-centeredness! That, we think, is the root of our troubles. Driven by a hundred forms of fear, self-delusion, self-seeking, and self-pity, we step on the toes of our fellows and they retaliate. Sometimes they hurt us, seemingly without provocation, but we invariably find that at some time in the past we have made decisions based on self which later placed us in a position to be hurt."[62] (Like shoving someone out of the salad bar line and then crying foul when they shove us back, proclaiming to anyone who will listen that *we* are the victim.)

• • •

One night before my discharge, after my three months in rehab, I made a promise in an AA meeting to a group of strangers who were oddly connected to me by our shared disease (but I didn't really know that yet, or, more accurately, I had not accepted my diagnosis of addiction). The realization that I was struggling under the weight of a brain disorder had not made that magical, million-mile trek from my head to my *heart*. On this night, my head was talking. The meeting was packed with hardworking, true-grit Texans, and I made my proclamation: "I promise to return home and do everything I have been taught and asked to do for one year. I don't think it will work. But I am dying doing it my way. I will get back to you with the results."

Even in my statement, I was proclaiming that I was a bit of an elitist, that I would lower myself to their level and methods of sobriety, that this Yankee would return home and prove them all wrong.

As it turned out, I proved them all right. I went to a meeting every day, found a sponsor, and worked the Steps. I was very afraid of my disease returning, and my fear was well founded when it comes to narcotic addiction. And science can explain this in part.

I've noted how opiate addiction has a much higher rate of relapse than alcoholism. You would think the converse is true, since alcohol is so easy to obtain on every street corner liquor store. So why is the recurrence rate higher for opiate addiction? Some studies tell us there is an analog in the brain that remembers "the high" of opiates, but that no such analog has been found for alcohol. This explains why the euphoric recall that occurs in the opiate addict can be so much more compelling than in the alcoholic. While statistics show that opiate addicts have a high rate of trauma in their pasts, especially sexual trauma, this is not true for every opiate addict. The truth is, we don't really know why people become addicted to certain drugs and not others. Genetics and brain chemistry certainly play a role, but my personal belief—and I have often seen this represented in the rooms of recovery and in my practice as an interventionist—is that a person's social environment plays a large role in the type of mood-altering drug he or she gravitates to. Health care workers such as me are familiar with and have access to opiates and other narcotics. Some professions have a higher prevalence of drinking alcohol as part of their networking and social atmosphere. This will exacerbate the problem for someone with the genetic predisposition toward alcoholism. Others have real chronic pain and are also addicts, and pain medication becomes the drug those individuals most commonly use. Then there are the street addicts, many of whom do not come from families of means; dealing and doing illegal drugs becomes a way of life and their social climate.

So when I returned home after those three months of rehab, I threw myself into recovery, the social network, working the Steps, and doing service work. Father Martin succinctly explained the Steps in a way I could understand, and Chris Raymer, a teacher at La Hacienda, echoed what I had learned earlier at Father Martin's Ashley rehab center.

First let me say that most healthy nonaddicts live the principles and practices represented by the Twelve Steps naturally. For us addicts, our emotional maturity is dwarfed due to our early use of mood-altering drugs, and our emotional lives are lived out like we are still kids. It's commonly accepted that our emotional development stopped at the age we were when we started using. This means that when we finally quit, we have a lot of growing up to do emotionally. The Steps, when put them into practice in the order in which they were written, can help us learn to live like responsible adults and accelerate our emotional maturation. The first three Steps teach us to believe in something outside of ourselves. For some this is a belief in God; for others, it is simply any Power greater than themselves, called a Higher Power in the program. For me, in the beginning, it was believing in the power of the group of people who surrounded me in the early days of recovery. It evolved over time. I now believe in a power of goodness and light that transcends this world. That power is not a guy in sandals with a long beard, but if that is your belief, that is wonderful. The power you tap into is one of your own choosing and can evolve over time. Hence the Steps are inclusive to everyone and their beliefs. This acceptance of all beliefs and faiths is a big part of Twelve Step recovery's ongoing success. The form that we envision the power to be is not as important as believing and depending on something outside of ourselves.

The middle Steps, four through ten, are about taking responsibility for our lives, righting our wrongs, living responsibly, leveling our egos, and continuing to monitor how we are living our daily lives and treating others. The last Steps are about continuing to grow in our relationship with a Higher Power and then passing it on to the next person.

We can know all of this and live it for a long time after coming home from treatment, but sometimes we get busy or distracted or complacent. That's when we can revert back to our addict behaviors, even while remaining abstinent from drugs. And if we have underlying emotional or psychiatric problems we haven't dealt with, the results can be fatal.

Suicide

Suicide. You hear it too often in the rooms of recovery, that people have committed suicide. And many people were sober at the time they killed themselves. A 2011 article in *Psychiatric Times* put it this way:[63]

> *Individuals with a substance use disorder (i.e., either a diagnosis of abuse or dependence on alcohol or drugs) are almost 6 times more likely to report a lifetime suicide attempt than those without a substance use disorder. Numerous*

studies of individuals in drug and alcohol treatment show that past suicide attempts and current suicidal thoughts are common. Recent evidence from veterans indicates that men with a substance use disorder are approximately 2.3 times more likely to die by suicide than those who are not substance abusers. Among women, a substance use disorder increases the risk of suicide 6.5-fold.

Another startling confirmation of the risk of suicide among alcoholics and addicts came in the 2008 report "*Substance Abuse and Suicide Prevention: Evidence and Implications*" from the federal Substance Abuse and Mental Health Services Administration: "A growing body of studies has demonstrated that alcohol and drug abuse are second only to depression and other mood disorders as the most frequent risk factors for suicide."[64] My friend and fellow addict Jerry was a case in point.

• • •

I loved Jerry. He was the kind of guy who would do anything for you if it was in his power. He had a keen sense of humor and found the light side of every situation. He made a mean cup of coffee for our early morning meetings. None of that cheap coffee found in recovery rooms—he always brought fresh-ground premium brew. He stayed close to a few male sponsors, but he continually went back and forth between them and his demon, heroin.

Jerry had a familiarity with guns from his many years of serving our country in covert special-ops missions. He spoke very little of his decade of military duty. I suspected it was not a pleasant time for him to talk about, and the secrecy was a commitment he made to his country. He had perfect eyesight and was a good shot. He said he had been presented with the Medal of Honor at the White House, but only the military knows why he received it. I think Jerry suffered post-traumatic stress disorder from his years of service.

He did joke about the intestinal dysentery he experienced in the jungle, and how it lingered even after he returned to the States. Maybe it was his experience with bowel issues that led him to help me out when I found myself in a disgusting situation. I was helping a fragile drug addict, hoping to get her into rehab. She had lost control of her bowels all around her living room before passing out in the basement. When I came into her house, her two dogs were making a meal of it. I am a nurse, but the sight and smell were overwhelming to me. So I called Jerry, the one person I knew would help me. "Jerry, oh my God, there is crap everywhere!"

He laughed. "That's it? Crap? What are you, a baby nurse?"

Well, yes, for most of my career I worked the nursery and neonatal care. "Please come and help me."

"You mean come clean up the shit for you? Okay, honey, hang on."

Within minutes, like an emergency hazmat team, Jerry showed up with all of the essential cleaning supplies, and he never flinched, gagged, or complained. He laughed. Jerry was always laughing, until his voice left us all.

I wish he would have called me when he needed help, but he called no one. After binging on heroin, Jerry would disappear. Concerned, I would go to his house, where I would find him on the couch, wrapped in a blanket, watching TV, and going through withdrawal. Lying ominously on the side table—and it was always the same after a binge—would be Jerry's revolver and two bullets, methodically placed with the flat ends on the table and the pointed ends facing the ceiling, seemingly waiting patiently for when Jerry finally hit the "jumping-off place." I never knew why there were two bullets; I assumed that if one did not do the job, he would have a spare to finish taking his life. I never asked him why there were two. Maybe I did not want to know.

Instead, I tried to reason with Jerry and make him see why he did not really want to commit suicide. "You will devastate your young son," I would implore. He never argued the point, but in the end, it did not deter him from leaving this world by his own hand. He did not use bullets, however. I assume he did not want to leave a mess for anyone to clean up.

One morning I got an urgent call from his ex-wife, Patty. "Have you heard from Jerry? He is missing," she said, her voice a mixture of anxiety and sadness, as if she already knew he had followed through with what we all suspected.

"No, I talked with him a few weeks ago," I said, already mentally beating myself up for not checking in on him sooner.

Later that day, Patty called me back. "We found his truck parked down by the Chesapeake Bay. His wallet and keys were locked inside." She went on as I silently listened, knowing I would never see Jerry again. "A sailor on the bay reported seeing him on his kayak. They exchanged words about the unseasonably warm fall day." The sailor thought Jerry's last words were about the weather, but most likely they were about his impending suicide: "It's not over until *we* say it is over." The sailor reported that forty-five minutes after those foretelling words from Jerry, he saw the kayak again—and it was empty.

First Jerry's kayak washed up to the shore. Then, ten days later, downwind on the Chesapeake shoreline, his body surfaced on the beach.

An autopsy showed no signs of a heart attack, stroke, or any other physical problems that might have caused him to go overboard and drown. Jerry was in good shape and most likely could have swum to shore if he had gotten separated from his kayak. His body chemistries did show an extremely high level of prescription opiates. My theory, like that of many others who knew of Jerry's consistent threat of suicide, is that he consumed a large amount of drugs and let himself drift to a watery grave. His wallet and keys, locked in his truck, seemed to indicate that he never planned to return to his vehicle. His death certificate cited "accidental drowning." I think the more accurate assessment of his cause of death would be "addiction," a chronic, progressive, and sometimes fatal disease. I think Jerry devised his death to look like an accident, leaving the real cause nebulous and open-ended for his loved ones. He was a kind man even in his own death.

In a 2002 article in the *American Journal of Psychiatry,* researchers reported that individuals who use opiates may have a noticeably higher risk of suicide than those who use other drugs. They add, "The findings also suggest the importance of distinguishing depression during abstinence as a risk period for suicide attempts. Clearly, remission of substance use is a welcome sign of clinical progress. However, special care may be needed to prevent suicide attempts in such patients, including careful review of the history of suicidal behavior and other risk factors for suicide as well as treatment of depression."[65]

In other words, addicts are at an increased risk of suicide during periods of abstinence and need to be monitored in this regard by their health care providers.

• • •

And then there it was, in my rearview mirror, *the grocery cart* I'd left sitting all alone in the parking lot. I stopped my van to look at it, and a vague but powerful nagging worry came over me. And then there were the times when it was raining that I was again parking my car on the "no parking, fire lane" curb, a regular practice when I was using. Everyone else could run into the store and get wet, but not me. Most troubling, my communication with people was becoming more and more entitled, and my newfound friendliness with strangers was now eluding me. The bitch was back . . . and I was "sober."

I told myself I was too busy for meetings, and I was busy, working as an interventionist, speaking, writing, and facing the challenges of raising two great kids on the autism spectrum. I had two learning curves, my own ongoing sobriety and my children's special needs. My marriage would take a hit, or maybe it had already taken too many hits, but it floundered and came to an end. I thought the hardest time of my life had come and gone—getting sober—but I was beginning to understand another hard truth: when it comes to pain in this life, it can always get worse. And it did. With my husband's abrupt departure from our home, I felt like I was losing another family, as I had with my family of origin, and old wounds from my past resurfaced. I felt like I was swirling down into a dark vortex. I wasn't using, but I was both subtly and powerfully seeing myself hanging dead in the closet. These thoughts would just pop into my head. My thoughts of leaving this world increased, but for the life of me (no pun intended) I could not figure out how to achieve my objective without hurting my kids. So once again my love for my children and their love for me saved my life.

Even so, just deciding not to kill myself was no way to exist in this world. Although I was off of drugs, something was way off in the already fragile state of my mind. The grocery carts I was leaving stranded in the parking lot continued to nag at my brain, and my dark moods began to scare me. In an attempt to assuage my fears, I started a new ritual.

One of the last projects my mom and I did before her diagnosis of lung cancer and death ten months later was to pick out material to have her two living room chairs recovered. When packing up her house after she died, I kept one of the newly covered pillows from the chairs as a keepsake, to remember our shopping days together. I use the pillow as a decorative piece on my bed by day, and at night I remove it from the bed before I go to sleep. As my dark moods escalated, I began to sleep with the pillow, resting my elbow and arm on it as I slept.

Sometimes in the middle of the night, my son Max will crawl into bed with me. I love it. His autism presents itself in that he does not easily kiss or touch much; his sensory system does not tolerate closeness. But at night, when he is asleep, he will cuddle up to me, and it is a gift to a mother whose arms ache for an authentic hug.

One night Max asked me, "Mom, why do you sleep with that pillow?"

"Well, Max, Grandma Mary and I picked out the material for the pillow together, and when the pillow is in bed, it is like having Grandma Mary with me."

His simple reply was, "Well, I guess she is sleeping between us."

I did not tell him the pillow was helping me feel safe. I did not want him to know the frailties I was feeling; he is supposed to depend on me to make him feel safe.

And then I got an unexpected gift. This was about the time I'd begun the long process of doing the research necessary to write this book and it scared the hell out of me. The theme I encountered over and over again was that it was not a matter of *if* my disease would return if I did not treat it, but *when*. And even more important, it had *already returned,* as evidenced by my dark moods and those damn grocery carts in the parking lot! I was on a major dry drunk.

So I dusted myself off and went back to meetings. That first meeting I stayed behind to talk to a girl who was pregnant and living in her car. I gave her phone numbers and resources where she could get help for herself and her baby. The room emptied out and it was just her and I. At that moment as I sat with this young woman, one addict talking to another, I realized working in recovery as a professional was not the same as working my own recovery program.

Within a week, my heart was lighter, and I felt joy and hope. I did ninety meetings in ninety days, just as if I'd actually relapsed and was using opiates again. I treated my "dry drunk" as if my disease had returned.

I am happy to report that I now return my grocery cart to the store sidewalk, and I no longer park on the curb. I am friendly to strangers and have stopped acting entitled. The bitch is in remission once again. But I still sleep with my mom's pillow.

• • •

In the last chapter, we will look at what researchers and others in the scientific community are currently saying about the disease of addiction. It is not all hopeful, but I think if you want sobriety badly enough, some of this information can help lead you in the right direction.

13

HOPE

Real Solutions for Improving
Opiate Addiction Treatment and Recovery

*It is often in the darkest skies that we see
the brightest stars.* • Richard Evans

Almost a century ago, the July 1919 issue of the *American Journal of Public Health* carried these words written by a Dr. Ernest S. Bishop.[66]

> *There is urgent need for widespread and early education of the medical profession, legislators, administrative authorities and laity into the facts of addiction-disease. Until narcotic addiction is widely appreciated and taught as a definite disease, and facilities are provided for clinical demonstration and instruction and for laboratory experimentation, we cannot hope for intelligent handling of the narcotic addict, nor for solution of the national drug problem. . . .*

As a definite clinical entity of physical disease, addiction is practically untaught in the school and unappreciated by the average medical man. . . .

In the light of available clinical information and study and in the light of competent laboratory research we are forced as a profession to admit that we have not treated our addiction sufferers with sympathetic understanding and clinical competency and that the blame for the past failure to control the narcotic drug problem rests largely upon the educational inadequacy of our medical profession, and institutions of scientific and public health education.

Again, that was in 1919, nearly one hundred years ago. In so many ways things have not changed, but this cannot keep us from trying, and that is the very purpose of this book—to keep the conversation going and to give practical advice to those suffering from this disease and to family members or other loved ones who know someone who is sick.

I think the reason change has come so slowly is that we addicts have a crappy reputation in the public's mind. I have often said society does not hate addicts and alcoholics for having the disease; it hates the wake created, the carnage that we leave as a result of having this strange affliction of the mind. People with many other diseases do not commit crimes to feed their illnesses, or kill innocent folks on the highway, or have unpredictable personality changes that result in domestic violence or, worse, the death of another. So there it is: we have a bad reputation. That, I believe, perpetuates the attitudes and perceptions about addicts and explains why not enough has been done to change the tragic fallout from this illness. I cannot change those facts, but I can give you practical tips and tell you how I, an opiate addict, am beating the odds and staying well.

Reforming Health Care

First, however, let me tell you what modern researchers say we need to do to increase the health and sobriety of addicts. Their proposals are not so different from what was written in 1919, although they do go into greater detail. Here are some highlights of the recommendations for reforming health care practice from the June 2012 report *Addiction Medicine: Closing the Gap between Science and Practice,* from the National Center on Addiction and Substance Abuse at Columbia University, that I believe are most relevant for policymakers and advocates.[67]

- Incorporate screening and intervention for risky substance use, and diagnosis, treatment, and disease management for addiction into routine medical practice.

- All medical schools and residency training programs should educate and train physicians to address risky substance use and addiction.

- Require nonphysician health professionals to be educated and trained to address risky substance use and addiction.

- Develop improved screening and assessment instruments.

- Establish national accreditation standards for all addiction treatment facilities and programs that reflect evidence-based care.

- Standardize language used to describe the full spectrum of substance use and addiction.

- Condition grants and contracts for addiction services on the provision of quality care.

- Educate nonhealth professionals about risky substance use and addiction.

- Identify patients at risk in government programs and services where costs of risky use and addiction are high.

- Develop tools to improve service quality.
- License addiction treatment facilities as health care providers.
- Require adherence to national accreditation standards that reflect evidence-based care.
- Require that all insurers provide coverage for comprehensive addiction care.
- Expand the addiction medicine workforce.
- Implement a national public health campaign.
- Invest in research and data collection.
- Implement the National Institutes of Health's recommendation to create a single institute addressing substance use and addiction.

I personally have not found a silver bullet from the medical community to keep me sober. Methadone and buprenorphine maintenance therapy intended to reduce my cravings for other opiates did not work for me. They *do* work for some people, as I stated in an earlier chapter. If your disease keeps recurring despite your best efforts, or if you have severe pain that cannot be controlled in other ways, then it may be worthwhile to try such therapies. But please understand that the detox process from methadone or buprenorphine can be tough and long for some and should be done under professional supervision. Both drugs have a long half-life, meaning they take a long time to clear the body. Naltrexone (Vivitrol), discussed in chapter 9, might be a better alternative.

Options for Getting Help

If you can't afford treatment and can't locate a program that will find the funds for a bed and you need a medical detox and have no insurance or other means, go to your local emergency room and tell them you need to be detoxed. Most ERs will accommodate you. To turn you away and have something tragic happen puts them in a bad liability situation. Once you have found your legs, go to your nearest AA/NA intergroup office and camp out. Someone will be answering the phones with whom you can hang out. Attend a meeting, raise your hand, and tell the group your situation. Someone will help you. What is true for AA is true for NA and the other drug-specific Twelve Step recovery groups: they are fellowships that exist to carry their messages of hope to those who suffer. Their members are in a unique position to help other sufferers, and they feel morally and ethically compelled to do so.

There are also Twelve Step meetings for family members and significant others. Al-Anon is the oldest, founded by Bill Wilson's wife, Lois; these meetings are held in every major city and most small towns. Nar-Anon also offers support for family members of addicts attending NA, and Codependents Anonymous (CoDA) is open to anyone who has developed a dysfunctional relationship with addicts or who has become obsessed with helping someone else as a way to compensate for a lack of self-worth.

If there is an office for adult social services in your area, call it and tell them your situation. Many times, state funds are available for people with no resources for addiction help. In my state of Maryland, such money is called Opportunity Treatment Funds (OTF). People with no resources are allowed one treatment in a lifetime. The catch is you have to be evaluated by state workers, and many times you are sent to outpatient treatment rather than inpatient care. But depending on the severity of your addiction and how long you've been using, outpatient treatment can be very helpful, especially if you are motivated.

In chapter 6, we talked about how many rehabs have either full or partial scholarship beds, meaning they are free or require only partial payment for treatment. Go to the Internet, look up treatment facilities, start calling, and tell them your situation. Also, you may be able to apply for no- or low-interest medical-necessity loans. Most rehabs have companies that they recommend. The payback period on the loans can often be deferred, giving you time to get back on your feet and working. If you have a retirement fund, many times that money can be used for medical emergencies with no tax penalty.

If you do have medical insurance but cost is a consideration, find out which rehabs are in your insurance company's network. Your insurance will pay a higher amount if you attend one of its "preferred" rehabs. Unfortunately, in today's climate, most private insurance pays for only a portion of inpatient addiction treatment. Many rehabs can give you a rough estimate of what you will owe when you give them your insurance and health information.

When the Twelve Step recovery movement began in the early days of AA in the 1930s and 1940s there were no rehabs. There were sanatoriums, but they were dismal places for people with mental illnesses. Folks in recovery could depend only on *each other* and working through the Steps with their sponsor in the order they were written, including doing service work and helping other alcoholics in practicing the Twelfth Step "to carry this message to alcoholics." Unfortunately, today, much of the knowledge of working the Steps and following through with a full commitment to attending meetings and helping other alcoholics and addicts has been watered down or lost. Too many recovery meetings have become more like support groups, where folks vent more about their lives than about the principles and practices of getting and staying sober as passed down from old-timers in the program.

I go to Big Book meetings where we read from AA's basic text that gave us the Twelve Steps and then discuss what we have read. Again, I transpose "alcohol" to "narcotics" in my mind. This helps to reinforce and illuminate how to *work* a program of recovery. I sleep with a "little" Big Book under my pillow. I know it sounds corny, but it reminds me every day of the disease I have. It is my medicine. I touch the book every morning when I wake up and am making the bed, and I say the Third Step prayer: "God, I offer myself to Thee—to build with me and to do with me as Thou wilt. Relieve me of the bondage of self, that I may better do Thy will. Take away my difficulties, that victory over them may bear witness to those I would help of Thy Power, Thy Love, and Thy Way of life. May I do Thy will always!"

If my day is really packed, I just touch the book and say, "God protect me." Sunny, my therapist at La Hacienda, insisted and *required* that everyone in her group say the prayer every day, and the first thing she asked us when we entered the magical room that was her office was whether we had said it that day. And she always knew when you were lying. How did she do that?

Beware of Cross-Addictions

In addition to being a disease of the spirit and emotions, addiction is also a biological disorder where addicts either don't produce enough dopamine naturally or lack enough dopamine receptor sites to absorb the dopamine produced naturally in their bodies. So how do we get dopamine without doing opiates?

One way some addicts do it is to switch from chemical addiction to what is called "process addiction", a compulsive behavior that does not involve drugs but still has been shown to produce dopamine in the brain. Such compulsive behaviors as people with process addictions, including Gamblers Anonymous, Debtors Anonymous, Sex Addicts Anonymous, and Overeaters Anonymous, which many addicts attend to supplement their AA, NA, or other drug-specific Twelve Step meeting.

Strategies for Staying Sober

To avoid developing process addictions and relapsing to opiate use, there are several ways I and other addicts have found that can not only restore the natural chemical balance in my brain, but also allow me to experience the lasting rewards of taking care of myself, emotionally and physically.

Exercise has been hugely beneficial to me. I have found that exercise in combination with energizing music increases my feelings of well-being and gives me energy to do other things that before felt like chores. And science supports this. Studies show that exercise stimulates brain cells that reinforce dopamine-related reward pathways. So every fall when the leaves change colors, the smell of fireplaces is in the air, and the euphoric recall of an opiate high is hounding my mind, I supplement my daily gym routine with an afternoon bike ride.

Laughter also increases dopamine levels. I have stopped watching "downer" TV and movies. I now consciously seek out funny and uplifting television shows and films. I am also fortunate to live close to a live theater that frequently books comedians. This does not come to me naturally. I tend to prefer dark subjects, murder mysteries, and intense drama that you can find all day long in theaters and on TV, especially with violence so prevalent in the media. But I now make a priority to seek out what is helpful to my state of mind rather than what will feed my addictive negative thinking.

Laughter not only improves my mood, but it increases my

optimism about life in general. The same can hold true for group sports; playing and listening to music; activities like painting, pottery, or carpentry; creative writing or just writing in your journal; dancing; hiking in a beautiful natural setting; and any number of other activities where you use your creativity and senses to meet your natural need for pleasure and creative fulfillment.

Those of us with co-occurring psychiatric disorders, like depression or anxiety, may need additional help in restoring our brain's chemical balance. I take antidepressants that increase serotonin, a cousin to dopamine. I shared earlier that I was diagnosed with general anxiety disorder with panic attacks and dysthymia, also known as low-grade chronic depression. It is very important to treat the mental illness diagnosis that so often accompanies a diagnosis of addiction. People whose mental illnesses go untreated are at a much higher risk of turning to drugs to self-medicate disturbing symptoms that occur with those illnesses. Getting professional help is vital to receiving the right diagnosis and, if necessary, the right medications to treat these disorders properly, which usually also involves "talk" therapy.

But the most effective thing I do to feel better physically, mentally, and spiritually is to work my Twelfth Step and help the next person. Helping others fills me with a purpose and—yep—there are some recent studies that suggest it probably also increases my dopamine levels. The truism really is true: "To the world you may be one person, but to one person you may be the world."

• • •

Help the next person—in the end, that may be the only real magic bullet. We do it not to be noble or superior, but to stay sober. We do it to help ourselves. Opiates are a powerful drug but they can't hold a candle to giving back to others what has been given to you. I hope you've found something in this book to strengthen your sobriety or to better understand your loved one's opiate addiction. If so, may you carry it forward to another addict who still suffers.

sober. We do it to help ourselves. Opiates are a powerful drug but they can't hold a candle to giving back to others what has been given to you. I hope you've found something in this book to strengthen your sobriety or to better understand your loved one's opiate addiction. If so, may you carry it forward to another addict who still suffers.

Your Plan for the First Five Days Sober and Drug-Free

This plan for your first five days is drawn from William Cope Moyers's book *A New Day, A New Life: A Guided Journal.*

Day One: Create a safe space

Your first recovery action step is to "trash your stash"—to clear your living environment of every last bit of alcohol or other drugs. Get rid of any materials (posters, music, shot glasses, phone numbers of using friends) that remind you of drinking or using. Don't do this alone. Ask your spouse, domestic partner, sober friend, or supportive family member for help.

You might be tempted to save part of your stash. Realize that this thinking will set you up for certain failure. Get rid of *all* your stash, and trust that you can let go of the need to control your life by using substances.

Write down the name of a sober person you can trust and schedule a time to meet to get rid of your stash within the next twenty-four hours. It's hard, but you can do it.

Day Two: Find a local Twelve Step meeting

Alcoholics Anonymous (AA) or Narcotics Anonymous (NA) Twelve Step meetings offer a fellowship where recovering people share their experience, strength, and hope. Going to AA meetings is especially important during the first year of recovery. You, like many others, may have felt isolated and lonely, as though you "didn't belong." Using alcohol or other drugs probably made that alienation even worse. What is the best cure for alienation and isolation? Friendship. When you make a connection with others in AA, loneliness will decrease. If you have a problem, question, or experience you don't understand, you can turn to a fellow AA member for help.

Use the Internet or your local phone book to find a Twelve Step meeting in your area. Make a commitment to go to a meeting during the next twenty-four hours, and plan to go at least once a week. Write down the address of the meeting and list the day and time you will attend.

Read the Big Book, pages 58–71 (fourth edition), "How It Works." Describe any fears or doubts you have about how the Twelve Step program can help you. Share these doubts in a Twelve Step meeting you attend this week.

Day Three: Find a sponsor

Twelve Step recovery is based on the idea that healing begins when you become willing to share your story with another person. In early recovery the first person you share with is called a sponsor. When you find a sponsor, you will have a special person who can listen to your story with attentive ears and an understanding heart.

Your sponsor will support, challenge, and help you in times of crisis and guide you through your Twelve Step work. It is not a sponsor's duty to keep you sober or take the place of a trained counselor; it is your sponsor's job to hold you accountable and assist you in building a healthy lifestyle.

When you attend your first Twelve Step meeting, make sure you don't leave without finding a temporary sponsor who is your same gender (or, if you're gay, of the opposite sex). A few people in your meeting will likely offer to be your temporary sponsor, but make sure you ask for help if you need it.

Your temporary sponsor will help guide you through the first few weeks or months of recovery. After you get to know people in your meeting better, you may always choose a different sponsor who better fits your needs. But right now make sure you identify someone who will be your sponsor. Program his or her phone number into your cell phone or keep it in your wallet.

Write down the name and phone number of your sponsor, and describe how you feel about having a sponsor to help you with recovery.

Day Four: Understand the brain science of addiction

Research has shown that addiction is not a matter of an individual's strength, moral character, willpower, or weakness. It has to do with brain chemistry and the way your brain is "wired." When you use drugs or alcohol, the chemicals quickly enter your bloodstream and, upon reaching your brain, trigger the release of feel-good neurotransmitters called "dopamine," which causes you to feel high. This feeling was so pleasurable that you wanted to repeat it again and again.

Eventually your body got used to the drug and needed more in order to feel high. What's more, your brain stopped producing feel-good neurotransmitters on its own. Ordinary things like exercise, sex, or even making a friend laugh no longer made you happy. Your body had become a hostage to the drug and you could not feel happy—or even normal—without it.

Your body was chemically out of balance, and your need to use was more powerful than your best intentions to quit. Because you couldn't quit, your drug use became progressively worse.

Can you relate to this description of how addiction progresses? Take a few minutes to reflect on your first use of alcohol or other drugs. How did your drug use progress? When did you notice that you needed the drug just to feel "normal"?

Day Five: Plan your day

In early recovery, you cannot be around any mood-altering substances. To stay safe, you will need to plan your day to avoid exposure to *all* people and places that could trigger you to use alcohol or other drugs. In particular, it's extremely important for you to stay away from bars or other places that remind you of using.

Don't fool yourself into thinking you can drink or use like your nonaddicted buddies, because you can't. Your brain is wired differently. Walking into a bar or meeting your using friends at a park is a "slippery slope" that will lead right back to drug use. Nonaddicts can have one drink and go home, but for addicts, one drink can easily turn into ten.

Think about the "slippery places" where you previously used alcohol or other drugs. Did you use when you were home alone? With friends? First thing after waking up in the morning? At concerts? Before or during a date? After payday?

List these slippery places and make a commitment to avoid them at all costs. Instead of going to a bar or over to a using friend's house, write out a plan to go to a Twelve Step meeting, connect with a sober friend, or go to a coffee shop or a bookstore.

Adapted from William Cope Moyers's *A New Day, A New Life: A Guided Journal* (Center City, MN: Hazelden, 2009). Used with permission.

The Twelve Steps of Alcoholics Anonymous and Narcotics Anonymous

The Twelve Steps of Alcoholics Anonymous

1. We admitted we were powerless over alcohol—that our lives had become unmanageable.

2. Came to believe that a Power greater than ourselves could restore us to sanity.

3. Made a decision to turn our will and our lives over to the care of God *as we understood Him.*

4. Made a searching and fearless moral inventory of ourselves.

5. Admitted to God, to ourselves, and to another human being the exact nature of our wrongs.

6. Were entirely ready to have God remove all these defects of character.

7. Humbly asked Him to remove our shortcomings.

8. Made a list of all persons we had harmed, and became willing to make amends to them all.

9. Made direct amends to such people wherever possible, except when to do so would injure them or others.

10. Continued to take personal inventory and when we were wrong promptly admitted it.

11. Sought through prayer and meditation to improve our conscious contact with God *as we understood Him,* praying only for knowledge of His will for us and the power to carry that out.

12. Having had a spiritual awakening as the result of these steps, we tried to carry this message to alcoholics, and to practice these principles in all our affairs.

The Twelve Steps of AA are taken from *Alcoholics Anonymous,* 4th ed., published by Alcoholics Anonymous World Services, Inc., New York, NY, 59–60.

The Twelve Steps of Narcotics Anonymous

1. We admitted that we were powerless over our addiction, that our lives had become unmanageable.

2. We came to believe that a Power greater than ourselves could restore us to sanity.

3. We made a decision to turn our will and our lives over to the care of God *as we understood Him.*

4. We made a searching and fearless moral inventory of ourselves.

5. We admitted to God, to ourselves, and to another human being the exact nature of our wrongs.

6. We were entirely ready to have God remove all these defects of character.

7. We humbly asked Him to remove our shortcomings.

8. We made a list of all persons we had harmed and became willing to make amends to them all.

9. We made direct amends to such people wherever possible, except when to do so would injure them or others.

10. We continued to take personal inventory and when we were wrong promptly admitted it.

11. We sought through prayer and meditation to improve our conscious contact with God *as we understood Him,* praying only for knowledge of His will for us and the power to carry that out.

12. Having had a spiritual awakening as the result of these
steps, we tried to carry this message to addicts, and to
practice these principles in all our affairs.

The Twelve Steps of NA are taken from *Narcotics Anonymous*, published by
Narcotics Anonymous World Service Office, Inc., Sun Valley, CA, 15–16.

Resources

Recovery Organizations

Alcoholics Anonymous: www.aa.org

Narcotics Anonymous: www.na.org

Heroin Anonymous: www.heroinanonymous.org

Pills Anonymous: www.pillsanonymous.org

Al-Anon Family Groups: www.al-anon.alateen.org

Nar-Anon Family Groups: www.nar-anon.org

Books

Basic Recovery Texts

Alcoholics Anonymous, 4th edition (New York: Alcoholics Anonymous World Services, Inc., 2001).

Narcotics Anonymous, 6th edition (Van Nuys, CA: Narcotics Anonymous World Services, Inc., 2008).

Narcotics Anonymous Step Working Guides (Van Nuys, CA: Narcotics Anonymous World Services, Inc., 1998).

Other Recommended Reading

Everything Changes: Help for Families of Newly Recovering Addicts by Beverly Conyers (Center City, MN: Hazelden, 2009).

Get Smart About Heroin: A Hazelden Quick Guide (e-book; Center City, MN: Hazelden, 2013).

Get Smart About Prescription Painkiller Abuse: A Hazelden Quick Guide (e-book; Center City, MN: Hazelden, 2013).

Heroin: Its History, Pharmacology, and Treatment by Humberto Fernandez and Therissa A. Libby, PhD (Center City, MN: Hazelden, 2011).

A New Day, A New Life: A Guided Journal by William Cope Moyers (Center City, MN: Hazelden, 2008).

Now What? An Insider's Guide to Addiction and Recovery by William Cope Moyers (Center City, MN: Hazelden, 2012).

Prescription Painkillers: History, Pharmacology, and Treatment by Marvin Seppala, MD, with Mark Rose (Center City, MN: Hazelden, 2010).

Recovery Now: A Basic Text for Today by Anonymous (Center City, MN: Hazelden, 2013).

White Out: The Secret Life of Heroin by Michael W. Clune (Center City, MN: Hazelden, 2013).

Alcohol and Drug Treatment Facilities: A Selected List

These are the alcohol and drug treatment facilities I respect and work with, listed in alphabetical order. Certainly there are other good rehab centers, but these are the ones I have experience with and trust to do a consistently superior job. For more commentary on rehab facilities, visit this book's Web page at the Hazelden bookstore: hazelden.org/bookstore.

Caron Foundation, 800-854-6023, www.caron.org
Caron Renaissance, 866-915-0290, www.caronrenaissance.org
Clarity Way, 877-251-6604, www.clarityway.com
Farley Center, 877-389-4968, www.farleycenter.com
Father Martin's Ashley, 800-799-4673,
    www.fathermartinsashley.com
Hazelden, 800-257-7810, www.hazelden.org
Kolmac Clinic, 301-589-0255, www.kolmac.com
La Hacienda, 800-749-6160, www.lahacienda.com
Mark Houston Recovery, 866-877-6080,
    www.markhoustonrecovery.com
Phoenix Recovery Center, 800-671-9516,
    www.phoenixrecoverycenter.com
Pine Grove, 888-574-4673, www.pinegrovetreatment.com
The Meadows, 800-632-3697, www.themeadows.org
Seabrook House, 800-761-7575, www.seabrookhouse.org

Notes

1. U.S. Department of Health and Human Services, Substance Abuse and Mental Health Services Administration (SAMHSA), Center for Behavioral Health Statistics and Quality, *National Survey on Drug Use and Health: Summary of National Findings,* Publication No. (SMA) 12-4713, Sept. 2012, www.samhsa.gov/data/nsduh /2k11results/nsduhresults2011.pdf.
2. Felix Gillette, "American Pain: The Largest U.S. Pill Mill's Rise and Fall," *Business Week,* June 6, 2012, www.businessweek.com /articles/2012-06-06/american-pain-the-largest-u-dot-s-dot-pill -mills-rise-and-fall.
3. Marvin Seppala and Mark Rose, *Prescription Painkillers: History, Pharmacology, and Treatment* (Center City, MN: Hazelden, 2010), Kindle Editions, Kindle Locations 1367–1372.
4. National Center on Addiction and Substance Abuse at Columbia University (CASA Columbia), "Behind Bars II: Substance Abuse and America's Prison Population," February 2010, www .casacolumbia.org/articlefiles/575-report2010behindbars2.pdf.
5. SAMHSA Center for Behavioral Health Statistics and Quality, *National Survey on Drug Use and Health: Summary of National Findings* (cited above).
6. Laxmaiah Manchikanti, MD, "National Drug Control Policy and Prescription Drug Abuse: Facts and Fallacies," *Pain Physician* 2007 (10:399-424), www.deadiversion.usdoj.gov/mtgs/methadone_alert /facts_and_fallacies.pdf.
7. *Alcoholics Anonymous,* 4th ed. (New York: Alcoholics Anonymous World Services, Inc., 2001), 152.
8. Margaret Warner, PhD; Li Hui Chen, PhD; Diane M. Makuc, DrPH; Robert N. Anderson, PhD; and Arialdi M. Miniño, MPH, "Drug Poisoning Deaths in the United States, 1980–2008," U.S. Department of Health and Human Services, Centers for Disease Control and Prevention, National Center for Health Statistics, NCHS Data Brief, No. 81, December 2011.

9. "Drugs, Brains, and Behavior: The Science of Addiction," National Institutes of Health, National Institute on Drug Abuse, NIH Pub No. 10-5605, printed April 2007, revised Feb. 2008 and Aug. 2010, www.drugabuse.gov/sites/default/files/sciofaddiction.pdf.

10. "New CASA Report Finds: 65% of All U.S. Inmates Meet Medical Criteria for Substance Abuse Addiction, Only 11% Receive Treatment," CASA Columbia, February 2010, www.casacolumbia.org/newsroom/press-releases/2010-behind-bars-II.

11. Source for this discussion of brain science: "Drugs, Brains, and Behavior: The Science of Addiction," cited above.

12. "Addiction Science: From Molecules to Managed Care," National Institute on Drug Abuse, July 2008, www.drugabuse.gov/publications/addiction-science/genes-environment-comorbidity/studies-have-shown-40-60-percent-predisposition-to-addiction-can.

13. Roger Highfield, "Drug Addicts Born Not Made, Say Scientists," *The Age*, March 4, 2007, www.theage.com.au/news/world/drug-addicts-born-not-made-scientists/2007/03/03/1172868811095.html.

14. "Why Do Some People Become Addicted?" HBO Addiction Project, www.hbo.com/addiction/understanding_addiction/14_some_people_become_addicted.html.

15. Ibid.

16. Lisa M. Najavits, PhD; Roger D. Weiss, MD; Sarah R. Shaw, BA; "The Link Between Substance Abuse and Posttraumatic Stress Disorder in Women: A Research Review," *American Journal on Addictions* (Volume 6, Issue 4, pages 273–283), Fall 1997; Article first published online, February 18, 2010, http://onlinelibrary.wiley.com/doi/10.1111/j.1521-0391.1997.tb00408.x/abstract.

17. *Alcoholics Anonymous,* 66.

18. Ibid., chapter 5.

19. This news story was widely reported in January 2013, including by ABC News, www.abcnews.com.

20. *Alcoholics Anonymous,* 24.

21. Donna Weaver, "Ocean County Surge in Heroin Deaths Spurs Action to Prevent Tragedies," *Press of Atlantic City,* June 9, 2013, www.pressofatlanticcity.com/news/breaking/ocean-county -surge-in-heroin-deaths-spurs-action-to-prevent/article _c589c892-d0b4-11e2-a16e-0019bb2963f4.html?mode=jqm.

22. Erin Marie Daly, "Heroin Deaths Surge in Fla. Following Pill Crackdown," Oxy Watchdog (blog), May 13, 2013, www .oxywatchdog.com.

23. Eliott C. McLaughlin, "Narcs Nab Drug-smuggling Puppies," CNN World, February 3, 2006, www.cnn.com/2006/WORLD /americas/02/01/drug.pups.

24. "Drug Facts: Heroin," National Institute on Drug Abuse, April 2013, www.drugabuse.gov/publications/drugfacts/heroin.

25. Leslie M. Shaw (Ed.), *The Clinical Toxicology Laboratory: Contemporary Practice of Poisoning Evaluation* (Washington, DC: American Association for Clinical Chemistry, 2001), 73.

26. "Heroin Statistics," Michael's House, www.michaelshouse.com /heroin-addiction/stats.

27. Ibid.

28. "Policy Impact: Prescription Painkiller Overdoses," Centers for Disease Prevention, December 2011, revised July 2013, www.cdc .gov/homeandrecreationalsafety/rxbrief.

29. State of New Jersey Commission of Investigation, "Scenes from an Epidemic: A Report on the SCI's Investigation of Prescription Pill and Heroin Abuse," July 2013, www.nj.gov/sci/pdf/PillsReport .pdf.

30. "Drug Facts: Heroin," National Institute on Drug Abuse, April 2013, www.drugabuse.gov/publications/drugfacts/heroin.

31. *Alcoholics Anonymous,* 102.

32. Laxmaiah Manchikanti, MD, "National Drug Control Policy and Prescription Drug Abuse: Facts and Fallacies," *Pain Physician* 2007; 10:399-424, www.deadiversion.usdoj.gov/mtgs/methadone _alert/facts_and_fallacies.pdf.

33. Thomas Francis, "How Florida Brothers' 'Pill Mill' Operation Fueled Painkiller Abuse Epidemic," NBC News Investigations, May 7, 2012, http://investigations.nbcnews.com/_news/2012/05 /07/11542417-how-florida-brothers-pill-mill-operation -fueled-painkiller-abuse-epidemic?lite.

34. "Top Pain Drugs in the United States Based on Revenue in 2011– 2012," Statista: The Statistics Portal, www.statista.com/statistics /242678.

35. Annual Report 2012, Grünenthal Group, www.grunenthal.com /grt-web/Grunenthal_Group/Company/Facts_and_Figures /124700099.jsp;jsessionid=7AAE2C8A01F95C14802F015BF F3AAD16.drp1. See also Barry Meier, "In Guilty Plea, OxyContin Maker to Pay $600 Million," *New York Times*, May 11, 2007, www .nytimes.com/2007/05/11/business/11drug-web.html?_r=3&hp&.

36. Annual Report 2012, Grünenthal Group, www.grunenthal.com/grt -web/Grunenthal_Group/Company/Facts_and_Figures/124700099 .jsp;jsessionid=7AAE2C8A01F95C14802F015BFF3AAD16.drp1.

37. "Policy Impact: Prescription Painkiller Overdoses," Centers for Disease Prevention, December 2011, revised July 2013, www.cdc .gov/homeandrecreationalsafety/rxbrief.

38. Jen Christensen, "Feds Boosting Mental Health Access, Treatment," CNN Health, November 8, 2013, www.cnn.com/2013/11/08/health /hhs-mental-health.

39. Revenue and CEO compensation figures are derived from company annual reports and/or business reports from *Forbes* and similar publications.

40. "Compare Substance Abuse Treatment Centers," Find the Best, 2014, http://findtreatment.samhsa.gov/TreatmentLocator/faces/services Search.jspx.

41. Mayo Clinic staff, "Fibromyalgia: Tests and Diagnosis," January 22, 2011, www.mayoclinic.org.

42. "Autism Speaks" (home page), 2014, www.autismspeaks.org.

43. Americal Psychiatric Association, *Diagnostic and Statistical Manual of Mental Health Disorders, 5th edition* (Bethesda, MD: American Psychiatric Association, 2013).

44. National Institute on Drug Abuse, "Prescription Drugs: Abuse and Addiction," NIH Publication Number 11-4881, Printed July 2001, Revised October 2011.

45. Richard Gazarik, "Use, Abuse of Suboxone Explodes in Western Pennsylvania," *TribLive*, Aug. 4, 2013, http://triblive.com/news /westmoreland/3938084-74/suboxone-drug-addiction#axzz 2pFxUgqwX.

46. *Alcoholics Anonymous,* chapter 8.

47. National Institute on Drug Abuse Research Report, "Prescription Drugs: Abuse and Addiction," www.drugabuse.gov/sites/default /files/rrprescription.pdf, 2.

48. "Assembly Bill No. 635," California Legislative Information, http://leginfo.legislature.ca.gov/faces/billNavClient.xhtml?bill _id=201320140AB635.

49. Roger Williams and Osvaldo Padilla, "Major Pain: Southwest Florida's Trouble with Opioids," *Fort Myers Florida Weekly,* March 14, 2012, http://fortmyers.floridaweekly.com/news/2012 -03-14/Top_News/Major_pain.html.

50. Russell K. Portenoy, quoted in Tina Rosenberg, "When Is a Pain Doctor a Drug Pusher?" *New York Times Magazine,* June 17, 2007, www.nytimes.com/2007/06/17/magazine/17pain-t.html?_r=2& oref=slogin&.

51. "Statement on Proposed Hydrocodone Reclassification from Janet Woodcock, M.D., Director, Center for Drug Evaluation and Research," U.S. Food and Drug Administration, Oct. 24, 2013, www.fda.gov/drugs/drugsafety/ucm372089.htm.

52. *Alcoholics Anonymous,* 24.

53. "Addiction Medicine: Closing the Gap between Science and Practice," CASA Columbia, June 2012, www.casacolumbia.org /templates/NewsRoom.aspx?articleid=678&zoneid=51.

54. B.P. Smith, J. Barry, E. Keenan, and K. Ducray, "Lapse and Relapse Following Inpatient Treatment of Opiate Dependence," *Irish Medical Journal* 103 (6), June 2010, 176–9, www.ncbi.nlm .nih.gov/pubmed/20669601.

55. "Sister Ignatia and Alcoholics Anonymous," *Barefoot's World,* www.barefootsworld.net/aasisterignatia.html.

56. *Alcoholics Anonymous,* 58.

57. Ibid., 23.

58. Ibid., 24.

59. Carole Bennett, "Is There a 'Dry Drunk' in Your Life?" *Psychology Today,* May 14, 2011, www.psychologytoday.com/blog /heartache-hope/201105/is-there-dry-drunk-in-your-life.

60. *Alcoholics Anonymous,* 64.

61. Sandra Cabot, Liver Doctor: Love Your Liver & Live Longer, www.liverdoctor.com.

62. *Alcoholics Anonymous,* 62.

63. Mark Ilgen and Felicia Kleinberg, "The Link between Substance Abuse, Violence, and Suicide," *Psychiatric Times,* January 20, 2011.

64. U.S. Department of Health and Human Services, Substance Abuse and Mental Health Services Administration, "Substance Abuse and Suicide Prevention: Evidence and Implications—A White Paper," Publication No. SMA08-4352, November 2008, http:// store.samhsa.gov/shin/content//SMA08-4352/SMA08-4352.pdf.

65. Efrat Aharonovich, Xinhua Liu, Edward Nunes, and Deborah S. Hasin, "Suicide Attempts in Substance Abusers: Effects of Major Depression in Relation to Substance Use Disorders," *American Journal of Psychiatry* 159:1600–1602, September 2002), www .columbia.edu/~dsh2/prism/files/EA_Suicide_attempts_AJP_1 .pdf.

66. Ernest S. Bishop, "Narcotic Drug Addiction: A Public Health Problem," *American Journal of Public Health* 9 (7), July 1919, 481–8.

67. "Addiction Medicine: Closing the Gap between Science and Practice," CASA Columbia, June 2012, www.casacolumbia.org /templates/NewsRoom.aspx?articleid=678&zoneid=51.

About the Author

Author of *The Interventionist,* **Joani Gammill** lives in Annapolis, Maryland, with her two children. She is in private practice working as an interventionist following a twenty-five-year career as an RN. A frequent guest on *Dr. Phil,* she enjoys speaking around the country on issues concerning addiction and recovery.

White Out

The Secret Life of Heroin

MICHAEL W. CLUNE

How do you describe an addiction to a drug that creates a hole in your memory, a "white out," so that every time you use it is the first time—new, fascinating, and vivid? Michael Clune's edgy memoir chronicles his life inside the heroin underground, leading readers into the mind of the addict and navigating the world therein. After his descent into addiction, we journey with him through detox, treatment, and finally into recovery as he returns to his childhood home. There his heroin-induced "white out" begins to fade.

Order No. 4678, ebook E4678

For more information or to order these or other resources by Hazelden Publishing, call **800-328-9000** or visit **hazelden.org/bookstore.**

HazeLDeN®

Hazelden, a national nonprofit organization founded in 1949, helps people reclaim their lives from the disease of addiction. Built on decades of knowledge and experience, Hazelden offers a comprehensive approach to addiction that addresses the full range of patient, family, and professional needs, including treatment and continuing care for youth and adults, research, higher learning, public education and advocacy, and publishing.

A life of recovery is lived "one day at a time." Hazelden publications, both educational and inspirational, support and strengthen lifelong recovery. In 1954, Hazelden published *Twenty-Four Hours a Day,* the first daily meditation book for recovering alcoholics, and Hazelden continues to publish works to inspire and guide individuals in treatment and recovery, and their loved ones. Professionals who work to prevent and treat addiction also turn to Hazelden for evidence-based curricula, informational materials, and videos for use in schools, treatment programs, and correctional programs.

Through published works, Hazelden extends the reach of hope, encouragement, help, and support to individuals, families, and communities affected by addiction and related issues.

For questions about Hazelden publications,
please call **800-328-9000**
or visit us online at **hazelden.org/bookstore.**